studios and lofts
ONE ROOM LIVING

First Published in the United States
of America in 2003 by

UNIVERSE PUBLISHING
A Division of Rizzoli International Pulications, Inc.
300 Park Avenue South
New York, NY 10010

2003 2004 2005 2006 2007 / 10 9 8 7 6 5 4 3 2 1

Printed in Spain
(Gráficas Iberia, s.a., Barcelona)

ISBN: 0-7893-0849-5

Library of Congress Catalog Control Number: 2002115846

Original title: Pequeños Apartamentos

© 2003 Gorg Blanc, S.L.
Via Augusta, 63
08006 Barcelona, España
www.gorgblanc.com

Editorial director: Jordi Vigué

Editor-in-chief: Sarah Kramer

Material and text: Marcos Nestares

Graphic design: Paloma Nestares

Publishing coordinator: Miquel Ridola

Documentation: Lee F. Vaugham

Photographic tractment: Albert M. Thuile

Translator: Lauren Hermele

Photographic collaborations:

Luís Asín (loft in Barbieri)
Bjorg (sjoberg)
Anna Blau (josefstadt)
Almond Chu (space + illumination)
Jean-Pierre Crousse (carmona, dc)
Didier Delmas (exclusive)
Santiago Garcés (carrer llums, poble nou,
malta, chimali, first work)
Graphein (garage)
Ryo Hata (seijo 6)
Markku Hedman (summer container)
Ros Honeysett (the grid)
Eduard Hueber (hill loft)
Sugino Kei (hakama)
Bruno Klomfar (box-studio)
Betsy Manning (darien street)
Ignacio Martínez (su-si & fred)
Daniel Moulinet (functional)
Patrick Müller (expansion, petits champs)
Paul Ott (hohe tauern)
Eugeni Pons (house in a suitcase, basic loft)
Alfonso Postigo (transformation)
Anne-Sophie Restoux (echard-baldwin residence)
Jenni Reuter / Juha Ilonen (straw house)
Makoto Sei Watanabe (atlas)
Philippe Seuillet (exclusive)
James Shanks (wilkinson mini-loft)
J. Vasseur (unique space)

studios and lofts
ONE ROOM LIVING

UNIVERSE

SUMMARY

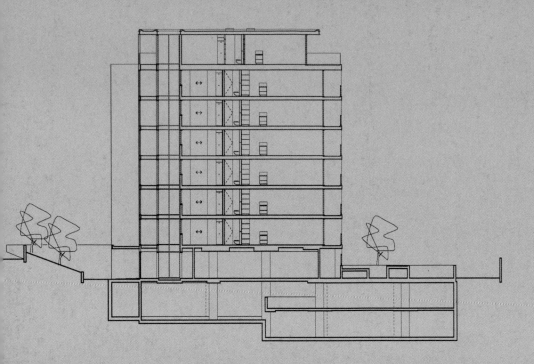

studios and lofts
ONE ROOM LIVING

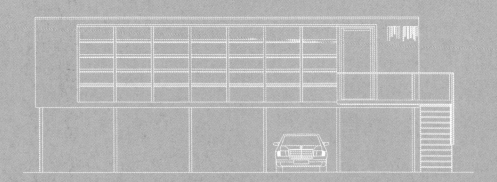

As the reader very well knows, architecture is an ongoing adventure that never stops evolving. Throughout history, just as with other arts, man has always been motivated by his eagerness to look for new forms, discover new paths, offer better provisions, and meet the reality of each moment. He is always researching and combining space and measurements, testing forms and materials, and making new proposals that are sometimes daring, sometimes functional, but always unique.

Inevitably, the book we are presenting today falls within this context. People's schedules and ways of life today and the lack of space and its corresponding inflation–especially in large cities–are determining factors that affect living spaces of the 21st century. The objective is to maximize the minimum, that is, to be able to offer, in a limited space, all the features that people currently need in their house, and aside from a modern design, to also present a pleasant atmosphere and a feeling of spaciousness–without neglecting comfort.

This book presents a select collection of designs that constitute an invaluable reference. Through them, the reader can see how many different architects from different countries, starting with very diverse suppositions (space, location, possibilities), have devised and developed their own solution faced with the same objective. Given that all the designs are all very recent (some have hardly just been finished), the contributions are quite varied, with styles that are sometimes diametrically opposed, and with materials, distribution, and concepts that are completely different. The great achievement of this volume lies in its variety and that it deals with current issues.

The selection has been carefully made from many choices, and this, as well as the preparation of the material and writing of the texts, has been taken care of by Marcos Nestares, a young architect, son of a family of various generations of architects, and outstanding author of numerous construction and remodeling designs of studios and small spaces in different countries–one of which happens to be included in this book, assuring its quality.

With great modesty but also with total sincerity, I am sure that we are offering the reader a work that, aside from its documentary value and being able to enjoy all the materials that are contributed, may also suggest different ideas that can be personally adapted.

The publication of this book was undertaken with this philosophy and objective. After seeing the result, our editing staff is convinced that we have accomplished our goal.

We offer you this book with our best wishes–there you have it; make good use of it and enjoy.

Jordi Vigué

VIENNA hohe tauern

LOCATION	**Vienna, Austria**
SURFACE AREA	**710.16 sq. ft.**
ARCHITECT	**Hans Peter Wörndl**
DATE	**1996**
PHOTOGRAPHER	**Paul Ott**

From the living room you can sense the presence of other spaces framed by the different lighting effects tested in this apartment.

The main premises of this apartment are: light filtration, permeability of the space, and the maximizing of corner areas.

A two-floor dwelling, the first floor is constituted of the living room and the humid areas while the upper floor is set aside for the bedroom and terrace area; both are joined by a staircase that, situated in the dwelling's center, distributes all the rooms.

This staircase divides the lower floor into two areas: one that accommodates the living room with exterior lighting–that diffuses out toward the rest of the floor–and another, formed by the hallway, kitchen, and bathroom, that does not have sufficient natural lighting. For this reason, the bathroom light is used to try to counteract the lack of light in this part of the dwelling; translucent glass unites the bathroom to the hallway, providing certain luminosity.

The living room's inclined geometry is taken advantage of to accommodate a large chink in the ceiling that, aside from connecting the two floors, constitutes a daily source of lighting for the living room, and a large nocturnal lamp for the bedroom.

Access is gained to the upper floor by a staircase (whose lighting makes it seem like it's floating) where there is a bedroom spatially joined to a multipurpose room, which flows into a large terrace with splendid views.

The predominant materials used in this apartment are smooth white plaster, for the walls and ceilings, and wood, for the floor, kitchen, and staircase.

A large triangular chink situated at the border of the living room ceiling suggests that an upper space exists, and also serves as a source of light for the apartment's main area.

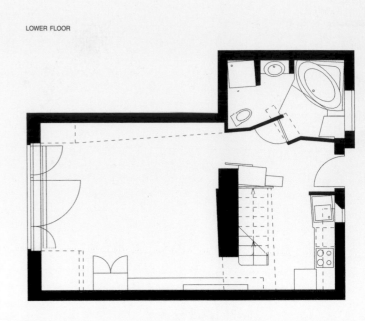

Two different spaces, joined by the staircase, are distinguished on this floor: one area with a humid center, and the large living room space served by the previous. A tendency of subtle broken lines is observed in the design's geometry–like those used for the bathroom's entrance–protecting the vision of access and helping with the orientation of its spaces.

The entire wall that separates the bathroom from the hallway and the kitchen is made of translucent glass–except for the most private area around the toilet. This system transmits diffused light onto the kitchen that lacks natural light.

The stairwell provides the transition between the kitchen and living room, and the luminosity from the upper floor helps to light the kitchen.

With just one small exterior window, the kitchen seeks light from both the living room and bathroom. To increase this effect, the main material used is light-toned wood. To make the most of all the apartment's corners, the architect placed a small desk for the kitchen under the staircase.

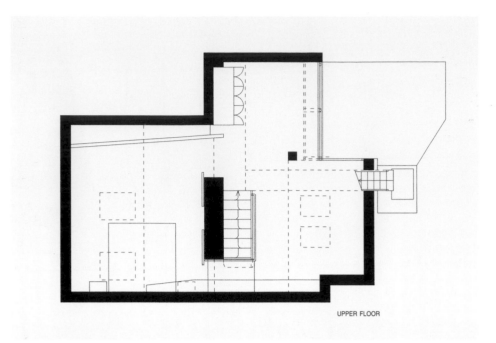

UPPER FLOOR

Situated on the top floor of the building, the apartment has a spacious open terrace area built with wood treated for exterior use.

There are three large rooms on this floor with the staircase as their central nucleus: the bedroom connected to the lower floor by a "fissure of light" in the framework, a studio area, and the anteroom of the exterior terrace.

There is also a chink of light on the completely wooden staircase that provides light to the lower area of the apartment, contributing to its lofty appearance.

The bathroom was created with gresite and ceramic walls that separate the different areas, and the walls were drilled with niches that serve as shelves. The metal and glass sink merges perfectly with the massive structure of the walls.

At night, the chink of light becomes a large lamp that illuminates the bedroom with the living room as its source of light.

BARCELONA house in a suitcase

LOCATION	**Calle Bruc, Barcelona, Spain**
SURFACE AREA	**290.52 sq. ft.**
ARCHITECTS	**Ricardo Flores / Eva Prats**
	Maria José Duch / Francisco Pizà
COLLABORATOR	**Frank Stahl**
DATE	**1997**
PHOTOGRAPHER	**Eugeni Pons**

This is a temporary apartment that has been conceived as a space in between a hotel room and a home. It is designed for people who travel and arrive to the apartment with limited luggage. The rest awaits them inside: two large trunks, like those previously used for long trips. When reaching this destination, the trunks are opened, and with this, each one can be transformed into furniture that contains everything necessary.

The room is closed most of the time, and a wide skylight that extends the whole longitude of the floor plan, illuminates its interior. When the owners arrive after many days away, they find a room flooded with light.

On each trip, a person brings a minimum of belongings with him/her. For this, the reduced space of the apartment does not allow for the buildup of objects. One of the objectives pursued in its design was to avoid the accumulation of dust during the times the inhabitants are away.

The project researches minimum space for daily activities; the furniture opens according to the needs of each moment of the day. Therefore the single 30 x 10 x 10 ft. room can vary in size and functionality throughout the day. In reality it is made up of two large units that relate its inhabitants to the room's space. When opening them, you realize why they are so large: according to how they are being used, hidden utilities are discovered in their different parts that fragment the large unit into human-size spaces with precise functions apt for daily activities.

In this manner, the signs of temporary occupation will be different for each stay, depending on the hand luggage that has been brought and the trunks that make up the room's furniture, which open according to the inhabitant's needs.

Before leaving the room, everything should be hidden again. The room's door is closed until the next visit, and the light and two large trunks are kept inside.

The criterion for the furniture unit's plan was the same as the trunks designed for big travelers of yesteryear. The architects thought of, for example, the compact closets and desks devised by the genius, Louis Vuitton.

Two large trunks, which store and generate all the utilities of this small apartment around them, are placed out of the way in a space 30 ft. long and 10 ft. wide.

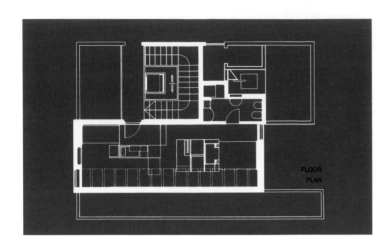

FLOOR PLAN

CROSS-SECTION

The apartment is made up of one main room; only a small adjacent area is reserved for the shower and bathroom. The space, which is longitudinal, is lit by a skylight, attached to one of the walls, which floods light into the entire room. Two large compact pieces of furniture are situated strategically apart that have many different uses when opened.

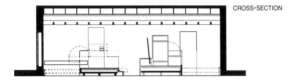

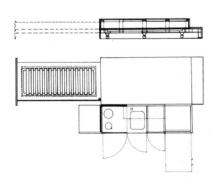

You can make shelves and resting tables appear in the kitchen furniture. An upper shelf prevents the kitchen from being seen from the entrance; a bed slides from under the shelf; and the wall becomes the backing for a sofa-bed.

FLOOR PLAN AND CROSS-SECTION
OF THE KITCHEN-FURNITURE UNIT

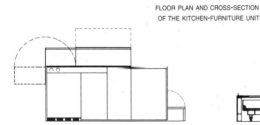

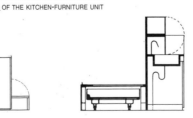

ISONOMETRIC VIEW
OF BED-FURNITURE UNIT

The furniture unit can be opened completely or partially, leaving the sink, work surfaces, and storage areas in view. You can also obtain a breakfast table with a closet for glasses and a pantry.

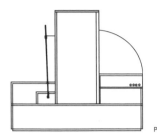

PERAL

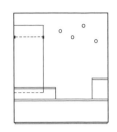

LUGGAGE
ELEVATION

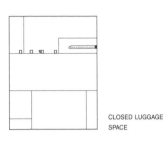

CLOSED LUGGAGE
SPACE

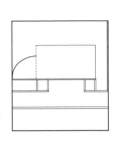

BACK ELEVATED
HEADREST

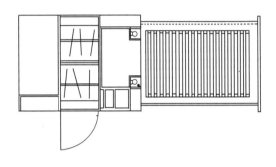

OPEN-FLOOR PLAN
BEDROOM FURNITURE

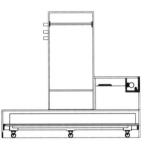

BEDROOM CROSS-SECTION

The furniture unit that is 22.596 x 17.216 x 20.444 ft. high, holds the apartment's double bed, which is hidden horizontally when it's not open. The vertical volume, conceived as a large headboard, accommodates the bedroom's typical storage zones.

The largest objects in the house, like the bed, to smaller objects are kept in the trunk with the larger volume. When one of the lids is opened, a flat, sliding tray appears to accommodate the smallest belongings, jewels, and pills. The furniture unit also has shelves for suitcases, a mirror, two small night tables with their own reading lamps and a drawer for the pillows and blankets.

The bedroom furniture unit contains all of the typical functions and storage areas for this space. The closet doors also make a folding screen, hiding the dressing area and achieving more privacy for the bedroom area, with the bed as the main component that hides in the unit's volume.

MONACO exclusive

LOCATION	**Monte Carlo, Monaco**
SURFACE AREA	**688.64 sq. ft.**
ARCHITECTS	**Claudio Lazzarini**
	Carl Pickering
DATE	**1997**
PHOTOGRAPHER	**Didier Delmas**
	Philippe Seulliet

This apartment belongs to a single businessman who occupies it just once a week; because he is alone, he always eats lunch outside.

The apartment–which interprets the client's desire to live in a continuous and free one-room space–was conceived by the architects as a first-class suite in a cruise ship over Monaco's sea, perfect for eating breakfast or having an aperitif.

A reinforced concrete shear wall divides the apartment into two linked parts: one contains the entrance, bathroom, and living room, and the other accommodates the bedroom, dressing room, bathroom area, and kitchen. Both flow into a large covered terrace.

The apartment's closets, mainly located in the dividing wall, were conceived as large translucent volumes that house colorful household items inside.

White floods the entire apartment and transmits functional and exclusive furniture.

From the seemingly independent terrace, the apartment's two main spaces–the living room and bedroom–dominate. A thick, reinforced concrete wall which accommodates the closets divides the two rooms.

The apartment's interior flows into an impressive room over the sea. Conceived as a limiting space between the exterior and interior, its low furniture was inspired by minimalist Japanese environments.

AXONOMETRIC

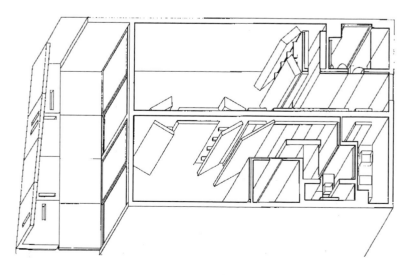

The two main spaces divided by a shear wall are compartmentalized from the inside to the outside, that is, from the apartment's inner entrance toward the large terrace over the sea. The utilities have also been segmented, assigning part of them to the most private area, forming part of the bedroom and dressing room, and another more public one that is made up of the living room and the main bathroom.

FLOOR PLAN

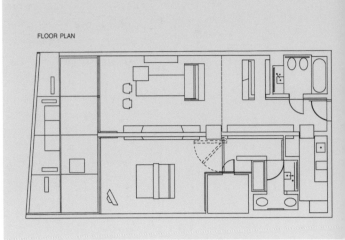

A studio of architects based in Rome designed this apartment; the Italian imprint is noted the smallest details. With an intention that was almost obsessive in the study of the closets, it is clear that the integration of this element is one of the most important values in an apartment with such limited space.

The closets and furniture, painted in a light tone like the entire apartment, are dotted with small color details that introduce a chromatic game into the design.

The closets that were installed everywhere, were conceived like light transmitters or reflective elements. They form sculptural volumes that hide the most fascinating surprises in their interior: a valued dish or an unexpected space.

The house's furniture uses the perimeter walls' white background as a canvas, mixing contemporary-designed furniture with others in an older style.

The large wall that demarcates the living room and bedroom is covered on both sides with a series of closets/shelves built with translucent material.

The bed is situated by itself in the bedroom area. As well as having an incorporated table that is very comfortable for reading or eating breakfast, it is finished off with a headboard with a large shelf.

The bedroom, also designed completely in white, transmits the same sensation of peace and quiet reflected throughout the apartment. Its line shows how comfort and design are not necessarily contrasting concepts.

Because this is a temporary house for a businessman who is almost always living somewhere else,
the bathroom and kitchen were conceived with
great simplicity, but always maintaining the
refined design that presides the entire plan.

Built in translucent glass or mirrors,
the closets' design makes them look
like floating sculptures.

KYOTO hakama residence

LOCATION	**Kyoto, Japan**
SURFACE AREA	**559.52 sq. ft.**
ARCHITECT	**Jun Tamaki**
	TAMAKI Architectural Atelier
DATE	**1998**
PHOTOGRAPHER	**Sugino Kei**

The two-level house is developed around a large central room, which, due to its large dimensions, is used for different purposes throughout the day –it can be used as a family room, a dining room, or simply as a play area for the children.

The exterior of this unique dwelling looks like a powerful white volume, a large vessel woven into a residential neighborhood of the city of Kyoto.

It contains a unique space inside, marked by the modern mentality of its occupants. The clients are a young couple with two children who wanted the dwelling to reflect their modern, different lifestyle, with the family united both physically and spiritually.

For this, the dwelling was devised around just one central space that could be used as a play area for the children, a dining room, or simply the environment in which the family's daily life would be carried out; it is a completely open space where the household chores and pleasure of a united family are shared.

With a height of 53.8 ft., its white parameters and large openings toward the exterior give rise to a sanctuary –a white open-plan room that prompts a great feeling of union and serenity.

Around this room, the surrounding space fades among the rooms all through the dwelling, which are simply demarcated by fine cloth partitions. These curtains allow for the air, light, and people to pass through them. With this delicate mechanism, the space can be converted into a large open-plan room, an environment in which the family can openly show its feelings.

The peripheral rooms, pierced in the large white volume, display crossed views from the central space toward the exterior–filled with the strength of a weighty monolith.

The exterior volume, more similar to the geometry of a religious building than a house, hides a valuable jewel inside: a monument dedicated to the family's unity. Its white monolithic aspect contrasts with its interior, marked by a very high space pierced by a large window, through which a diffused light penetrates and bestows on the room an almost sacred character.

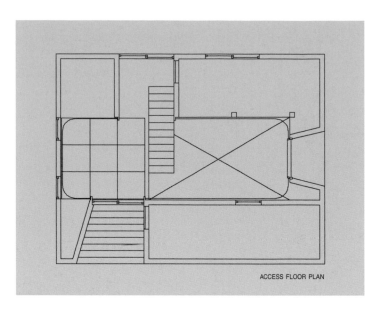

ACCESS FLOOR PLAN

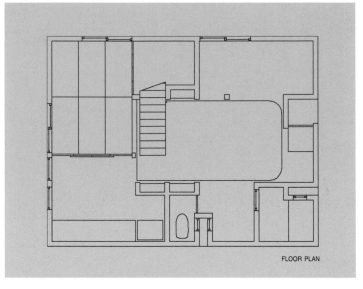

FLOOR PLAN

A few large curtains demarcate the necessary rooms in the house. Through this lofty separation, the house's space can be converted into one open-plan and united space or into different independent rooms.

The natural light, coming from a big opening pierced in the facade's large volume, fills all the parameters of the dwelling, reflecting an atmosphere of peace and serenity.

The curtains that separate the rooms
are traversed by the light, people, or
simply by the air, which transforms
the dwelling into a building where
the crossed views and circulations
among the rooms create a great
feeling of spaciousness and unity.

PHILADELPHIA darien street

LOCATION	**Darien Street, Philadelphia, Pennsylvania, United States**
SURFACE AREA	**710.16 sq. ft.**
ARCHITECTS	**Michael Bucci**
	Angela DiPrima Bucci
DATE	**1998**
PHOTOGRAPHER	**Betsy Manning**

The existence of an apartment with five separate sealed rooms was what the design started with. The new renovation maintained these rooms but established a visual and spatial flow among them that enriches the space.

The interior distribution is clear and simple: a large space that accommodates the kitchen and living room, and a more private zone formed by two rooms, a bathroom, and a storage area.

The diffusion of the light is a principle element for interconnecting the rooms. A few horizontal strips of glass, constructed on the upper part of the walls, dissolves any clear separation between the spaces and spreads the light between each room and its annex–while maintaining the necessary privacy. With a skylight above the shower, the interior bathroom was constructed like a large pool of light that illuminates the apartment's darker parts. In this fashion, the ritual of the morning shower also seems to acquire a spiritual connection with the sky.

The artificial lighting, like the natural lighting, was studied, offering different zenithal suspended skylights.

The treatment of the materials, the industrial lighting, and the exposure of the structure's beams give the apartment an industrial image of a small loft.

The kitchen takes up a large corner next to the entrance. Its furniture, with an abundance of drawers and volumes, is integrated into the wall, therefore forming one face. The exterior window is framed between the closets, and the whole unit forms a compact greenish-gray-toned block.

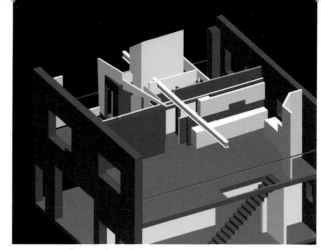

A small, medium-high wall protects the immediate view of the staircase that forms the apartment's entrance. The iron railing was maintained, giving the apartment a rustic touch with an industrial aesthetic.

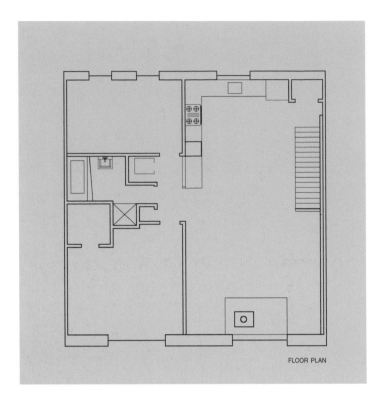

FLOOR PLAN

The apartment is divided almost mathematically into two segments: one is occupied by a large main living space, joined with a spacious kitchen, and the other distributes the bathroom, the storage areas, and two spacious bedrooms.

As a counterpoint to a so-called coldness in the treatment of the space, a small chimney was placed in the living room's corner.

As with the stairway, the bathroom is protected from being seen immediately by a small, medium-high wall that does not break up the spatial continuity.

The hall that accesses the bedrooms
and bathroom, a theoretically darker point,
turns into a space flooded by light from the
continuity established between all of the rooms.

Both bedrooms are connected to the living room's main space by a strip of glass situated on the upper part of the wall. This preserves the necessary privacy, but also maintains the luminous continuity strived for in the entire design.

The industrial image is maintained in the bathroom with fluorescent tubes, industrial skylights, and exposed structures, trying at all times to show the apartment's real construction and granting it the image of a loft. A zenith skylight, which becomes a large pool of light for this room and its annexes, lights up the bathroom located between the bedrooms.

HONG KONG space + illumination

LOCATION	**Hong Kong, China**
SURFACE AREA	**322.32 sq. ft.**
ARCHITECTS	**Gary Chang / EDGE (HK) LTD.**
DATE	**1998**
PHOTOGRAPHER	**Almond Chu**

To tone down the floor's rigidity and make it more ethereal, fluorescent tubes and a bright light were installed that articulate the structural elements.

Here we have an efficient studio that has obtained a varied plan in this reduced space.

The spatial flexibility was created through different operations and resources, such as partitions, lighting, and furniture. All of the household equipment for a single person (books, CDs, hall, wardrobe, paintings, audio and video equipment) is stored on an industrial-like chromium-plated bookcase, hidden discreetly behind a light white curtain.

As a contrast, there is a compact wooden unit that incorporates all the fixed elements: bath, kitchen, washing machine, heating unit, and video projector.

The central space is, in reality, the area for: living, working, eating, sleeping, getting dressed, and being.

A blue fluorescent light has been carefully hung to bathe the floor, and some white lights articulate the apartment's elements at the level of the ceiling. All these are variables according to the activity performed to obtain a relaxed and lucid environment.

The predominance of white, translucent elements, and transparent materials, combined with a changing environmental light seem to make the entire apartment vanish.

The large mobile movie screen, located on the main window, offers different views of the world: the fantasy of Hollywood, the daily world news, or the virtual universe of Internet.

This apartment located in a neighborhood of Hong Kong stands out, faced with the apparent chaos and traffic in this cosmopolitan city where the square meter has to be inescapably maximized.

In order to make the most of the apartment's largest source of natural light, the bathroom and kitchen are located in the front area. Therefore, the main space remains free for the different activities that take place throughout the day; light partitions, furniture, and shelving are used along the apartment's perimeter.

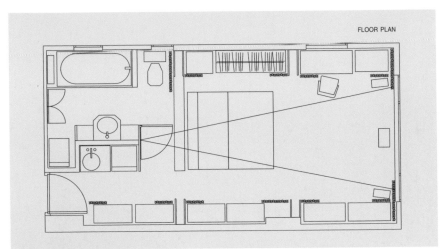

FLOOR PLAN

All the worldly implements of a single person (books, CDs, wardrobe, paintings, audio and video equipment) are stored in an industrial-like chromium-plated bookcase, hidden discreetly behind a light white curtain.

In this apartment, all household equipment and the inhabitant's wardrobe may remain hidden depending on the different times of day. The treated lighting brings a lofty aspect to the apartment in which the material seems to disappear.

A sculptural piece of furniture that houses the kitchen and bathroom was created as a solid cherry wooden tower, standing out in an environment in which white is the predominant color.

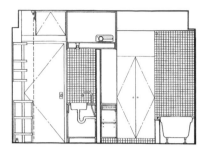

CROSS-SECTIONS

The careful study of the cross-section perfectly fits together with the nucleus of fixed elements, where even a film-projecting screen is included. This way, the most is made of a minimum space.

In this reduced-dimension bathroom, great expressiveness is achieved, combining design elements like the Phillippe Starck faucet with more economic solutions for the lighting with a base of fluorescent tubes.

The entrance area is taken advantage of to house a piece of kitchen furniture where necessary utensils and a small refrigerator are kept.

The bathroom has been divided into two parts: one
accommodates the bath and the other the toilet, which is hidden
from the main space by a medium height bookcase and a curtain.
In this manner, the bathroom zone can remain equally isolated
or be visually included in the apartment's single space.

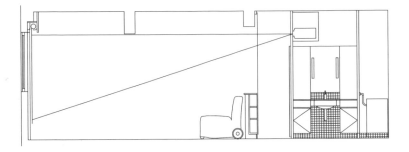

In these sections, the two elements that make up the plan are appreciated: the compact area of the kitchen and bathroom that frees up the rest of the space, with shelving adjacent to the walls for the storage zone.

LONGITUDINAL SECTIONS

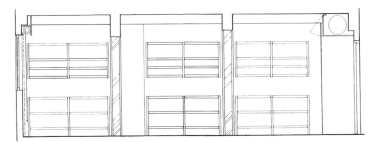

A low wall–also a bookcase–visually separates the toilet area and spatially connects it to the bathroom, making the apartment into one space with lighting that changes according to the function and time of day.

The apartment's transversal window offers the possibility to convert this into a projection room where the fantasy of Hollywood lives along with the real world through the news, or the infinite world of the Internet.

PARIS expansion

LOCATION   **Avenue de Choisy, Paris, France**
SURFACE AREA   **269 sq. ft.**
ARCHITECT   **Guilhem Roustan**
DATE   **1998**
PHOTOGRAPHER   **Patrick Müller**

This small studio faces the terrace by means of a glazed parameter around the frontal part of the terrace, constituting its main space.

This apartment is the fruit of an apartment building expansion surrounded by two level constructions.

The project consisted of erecting a new construction on top of the already existing one to be able to free up the view and open the panorama above the Paris rooftops, with the 13th arrondissement apartment buildings as a backdrop.

The floor plan also carries out the functions of the bedroom, office, and bathroom, around a shower and closet block–the corresponding space takes advantage of the depth of the other for each function.

A wall with a large window that continues to the upper part separates the exterior, letting the light in and freeing the interior of the apartment from the chaotic view of an adjoining patio.

This wall and the articulation of the roof's flatness compress the space, accentuating the horizontality and extending the space toward a terrace. The terrace is oriented toward the south, and thanks to the system of sliding doors with shutters, it becomes an exterior space integrated into the patio and protected from sight.

The architect did not want to conceive this as a construction juxtaposed to the building, rather he wanted it to be the improvement of one uninteresting exterior façade–creating a dynamic and modern continuity for the recomposing of the existing structure.

The architect composed the new façade as if dealing with an entirely new element; he does not follow the norms of the previous construction, giving it a more rational air where the windows are a product of interior activity. However, he used old and contrasting systems, shutters to shade the light and vision. The partial elevation of the building allows for the wide opening of the patio space, which permits for a splendid view over the existing rooftops.

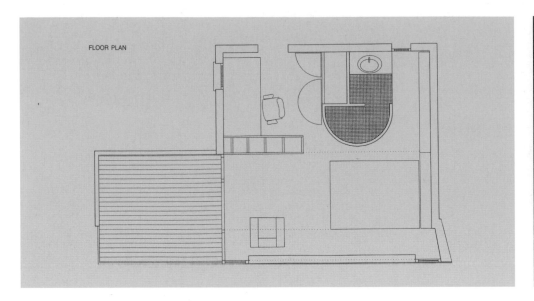

FLOOR PLAN

The shower's curved parameter located between the entrance and the bath, orders the surrounding space, preventing the bedroom area from being seen immediately. This curved gesture helps to spatially read how the apartment is used.

A 24.31 ft.-high wall limits the direct view onto the chaotic patio. The only lighting in the room is provided by a sliding window in the wall at ceiling height and two small vertical borders of glass for a partial view of the patio.

The glass enclosure, the dividing neighbor wall, and the lengthening of the cover that compositely connects with the interior volume demarcate the terrace.

The shower is built entirely of gresite in a sculptural curve that articulates the living room and bedroom.

An exterior frame separated from the
wall/screen by a system of metallic
columns, allows the sun that enters from
the South to be captured, and makes the
bedroom's space larger toward the terrace.

On the terrace, the shutter
system tends to erase the limit
between the interior and
exterior: it allows for fragments
of the landscape over the Paris
rooftops to be seen, which the
spectator should rebuild.

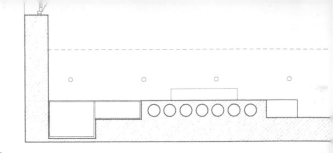

PARIS APARTMENT carmona

LOCATION	**Rue de Turenne, Paris, France**
SURFACE AREA	**344.32 sq. ft.**
ARCHITECTS	**Sandra Barclay / Jean Pierre Crousse**
DATE	**1999**
PHOTOGRAPHER	**Jean Pierre Crousse**

All the details have been carefully studied. From the hall all the spaces that make up the apartment can be sensed, and a vertical opening in the quartering of the closet suggests what lies on the other side.

This small apartment is found in the Marais neighborhood in Paris, and is part of a building from the 18th century.

Its reduced dimensions and the difficulty of a large cargo wall that divides it in two oriented the project toward the space's expansion. This space has been freed from partition and unnecessary walls to make the apartment as spacious as possible.

The authors of this plan believe that intervening in a reduced space requires as much effort as needed for a work of great magnitude. The definition of a project strategy is essential to change these spaces into livable and comfortable spaces.

In accordance with this, the new elements added to the original structure have been conceived in a way so that the furniture reveals independence between the historical structure and contemporary intervention.

The distribution in this minimum space has been derived in an absolutely rational way. There is a small entrance hall that is distributed toward the bathroom, bedroom, and living room where an open kitchen attached to the wall that divides the apartment in two is located.

All the parameters and furniture are white to highlight the luminosity and to reinforce the feeling of spaciousness.

The historical architecture of wood load-bearing walls and a modern conception of an open and unified space coexist in this project, in both functions and materials.

The distribution is conditioned by the load-bearing wall, which divides the apartment into two spaces. This is taken advantage of to attach the kitchen exposed to the living room. The rest of the vertical parameters have been distributed with a clear interest in making the most of the space.

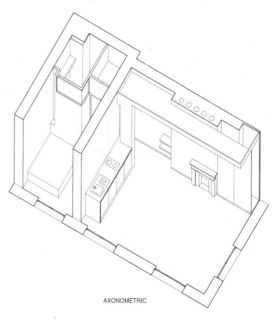

AXONOMETRIC

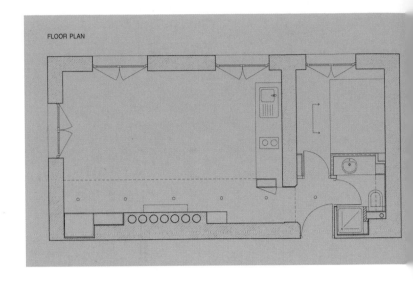

Every nook and cranny of the apartment has been made the most of to fit the necessary elements of an apartment that, in spite of its reduced dimensions, is fully equipped. Therefore, in the bathroom, the shower has been placed to take advantage of an imperfection in the existing wall.

The floor tiles and original wood beams have been maintained from this old building. White has been used on the rest of the parameters and furniture to increase the luminosity of the dwelling.

The kitchen, open to the room, has been designed like a piece of furniture of pure forms that leans against the vertical parameter, which horizontally breaks to show the path from the entrance to the chimney, the prevalent feature of the living room.

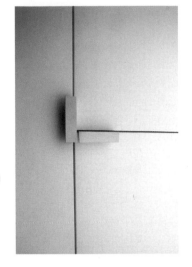

All the closets and their quartering have been carefully designed by the architects up to the smallest details, like the metallic profile made by the handles.

In spite of being located in the dwelling's darkest area, the bathroom receives a halo of luminosity from the upper part of the glass parameter that separates it from the bedroom.

In spite of its reduced dimensions, the bathroom is fully equipped; all the corners have been made the most of for storage zones. All the parameters and furniture are white to favor the feeling of space–the large mirror in the bathroom area also contributes to this.

TRANSPORTABLE su-si & fred

LOCATION	**anywhere (Germany)**
SURFACE AREA	**SU-SI 376.59 sq. ft.**
	FRED open 193.68 sq. ft.
	closed 96.84 sq. ft.
ARCHITECT	**Oskar Leo Kaufmann**
DATE	**1999**
PHOTOGRAPHER	**Ignacio Martínez**

SU-SI and FRED are an interesting German response to the demand these days for housing characteristic of a global world: economic, adaptable to any environment, and transportable.

Neither of the two exceeds 376.59 sq. ft., and include everything of a minimum-size apartment (bedroom, living room, bathroom, and kitchen). Aside from acting as a space for a couple, or a vacation residence, these mobile units can be used for other very different functions: business office, studio, construction work office, etc.

Their design has been carefully studied to maximize the minimum space while providing optimum living conditions.

The prefabrication in the workshop, that would not surpass five weeks, also managed to minimize the costs from any conventional construction.

These dwellings can be transported by tow-trucks and installed on an *in situ* foundation. The only condition is that the site has must have electricity and water connections and an evacuation route for waste.

Its neutral aesthetic is premeditated so that it can be located anywhere.

FRED goes even further with the concept of a mobile living space since its 96.84 sq. ft. is able to expand up to 193.68 sq. ft. once installed in its location, minimizing transportation costs.

These two living spaces conceptualize the living space as a transitory consumer product, like a washing machine, car, etc.

Wood is the main material used. The workshop production minimizes costs and provides better quality control, eliminating the inconveniences of conventional construction work. The location's preparation only requires provision of water, electricity, and the existence of a drainage system, as well as the construction of a simple metallic or concrete foundation.

FRED's uniqueness is in the possibility of being collapsed into one size, cutting its dimensions in half, with subsequent savings on transportation.

SU-SI, created in a white tonality, has an abstract and neutral component that enables it to be located on any site without standing out or competing with the environment.

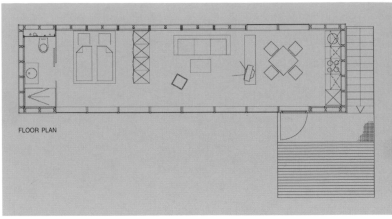

FLOOR PLAN

The installation process on the site, which doesn't take longer than five hours, is performed by medium a tow-truck (because it doesn't weigh more than twelve tons).

Markedly longitudinal, the floor plan is organized with continuity, situating the fixed bathroom and kitchen zones on the smaller sides, therefore freeing the rest of the space organized to the consumer's liking.

The vertical parameters visually expand the dwelling toward the outside, making it seem larger.

The entire interior, including the roof, has been built with light-toned wood, which favors the outside luminosity. The light is diffused by a brisoleil reticle that protects the interior from the direct sunlight and also serves as shelving.

The modular system of the prefabrication reduces the costs and simplifies its production in the workshop.

SU-SI's beautiful nighttime image confers it an abstract element that makes it seem to float in space, like a ship appearing in town which tomorrow might be gone.

The furniture is composed of unattached elements within the dwelling's unit. To complement the continuity the different atmospheres are separated with furniture that does not reach the ceiling.

LONGITUDINAL SECTION

LONGITUDINAL SECTION

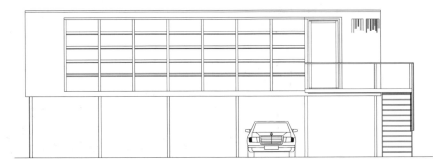

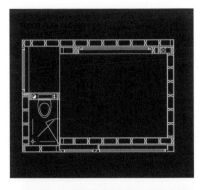

FRED is a 105.94 cubic ft. living space when closed. When opened it reaches 193.68 sq. ft. This is possible due to the electronically controlled sliding walls on rails. In the interior there is a small free room, a fully equipped kitchen, bathroom, and shower.

After arriving of the settlement, FRED can be opened electronically by the user, them connected to the water and electricity supply. Obviously, the furniture and other elements can remain in the unit.

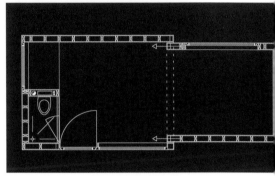

The large glass front provides the
room with natural light. The quality of
the materials and the thick insulation
of the walls, roof, and floor minimize
the loss of heat. The use of wood and
glass as the only materials create a
positive impression, making it possible
to blend in with any environment.

NEW YORK hill loft

LOCATION	**New York City, New York, United States**
SURFACE AREA	**720.92 sq. ft.**
ARCHITECTS	**Joseph Tanney**
	Robert Luntz
DATE	**1999**
PHOTOGRAPHER	**Eduard Hueber**

The alteration of a space in an old industrial building in Manhattan gave rise to a small open-plan loft with a spacious: kitchen area, bar, sleeping area, and relaxation area.

The architects took advantage strict modulation of the structure to accommodate the different rooms, placing a large front area for storage between the pillars and attached to one of the walls, therefore freeing up and accenting the rest of the space.

A small hall can be accessed from the entrance that is protected by a set of shelves that do not reach the ceiling, therefore extending the view.

The kitchen opens out into the living room and the storage area is made the most of placing closets, electrical appliances, and household equipment. It has a table island as a work surface and another table next to it for dining; these two complementary elements constitute a unitary area.

The living room is completely clear of any conventional partition walls, favoring more simple and functional furnishings that are dealt with very lightly so as not to overwhelm a fairly limited space.

There is a large sliding door integrated into the shelving that grants access to the most personal area of the apartment.

A few curious, winding, intertwined lights are situated on the ceiling that is preserved from the old building. The incorporation of diffuse lighting emphasizes the building's structure and its relation to the large frontal area of shelves.

Wood and steel are the primarily used materials that contrast with the white structure of the old building.

The good natural lighting from the two large windows and the view of a Manhattan street make this loft spacious and cozy.

From the entrance, flanked by a set of shelves, you can see the entire depth of the apartment that seems more spacious than it really is because there are no interior partitions. The kitchen is in the foreground, and further away, the relaxation area next to a large window that lights the entire loft.

This loft is located in a typical Manhattan building. Its industrial precedents have equipped it with very high ceilings that are excellent for the new residential use of its interior space.

The sturdy metallic structure of the riveted beams and pillars was left exposed and painted white. There is a front area of shelves for the storage of household equipment and electrical appliances situated along one of the walls. This contrasts with the metallic structure and frees up the rest of the surrounding space.

There are three basic chromatic tones in this apartment: white for the structure and parameters, wood for the furniture and floor, and metal for various elements like the entrance door, the refrigerator, and suspended lights.

The suspended lights wander the ceiling, visually joining the apartment's areas. Their design contrasts with the old factory's ceiling molding.

The sturdy pillar capitals remain from the old decoration and were left visible so that the apartment maintains an industrial feel, characteristic of many lofts.

The kitchen area was integrated into the large front area of shelves. Its strongly rational design makes the most of all the corners to accommodate the largest amount of shelves and drawers. Wood and steel are used, offering an industrial vision that is very appropriate for a loft.

The kitchen is equipped with a large work surface island with a large amount of compartments and drawers, and an extractor hood located above. This whole area forms a sculptural block that is largely prominent in the apartment.

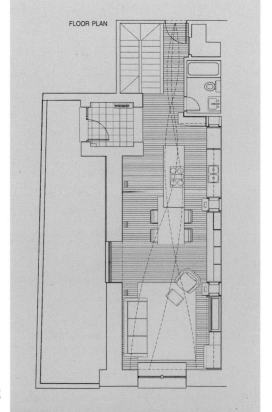

FLOOR PLAN

The result of combining the different spaces gives rise to a relaxed and spacious atmosphere with different possible uses.

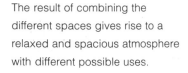

The dining room area with the prolongation of the kitchen island table, projects the longitude of a room with an already good depth.

The bedroom is hidden behind a sliding door inlayed on the front area of shelves. Facing the living room, they can visually make the space larger, also favoring its ample luminosity. The living room is made visually larger thanks to simple and functional furnishing, strategically placed so as not to compress the space.

The thick wall, fundamental to the project, takes in the chimney's ducts and the loadbearing elements. In this wall, a new window was created to visually link the main room to the foyer.

The concrete framework, situated below the roof in interstitial spaces and damp areas, presents a smaller, more human scale that contrasts with the high ceilings in these old buildings.

The main room of rectangular proportions forms an open-plan space that can be used as a living room or a bedroom. Its large amount of lighting also contributes to a sense of spaciousness.

The kitchen, located next to the spacious entrance hall, can be integrated or separated from the hall by a large sliding panel, therefore compressing or expanding the space.

Starting with two small apartments with a compartmentalized distribution, typical of buildings from the 19th century, a fluid, modern apartment was obtained where the spatial limits vanished. Two main spaces are distinguished in the new apartment. One, situated in front of the patio, is made up by the entrance, kitchen, bathrooms, and storage areas; and the other, facing the street, furnishes a room with a sliding panel that separates the most private area of the apartment.

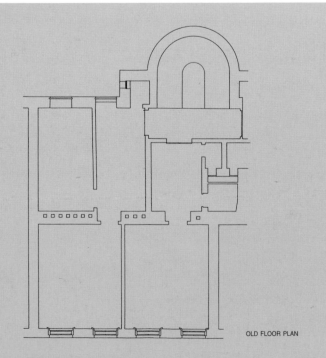

OLD FLOOR PLAN

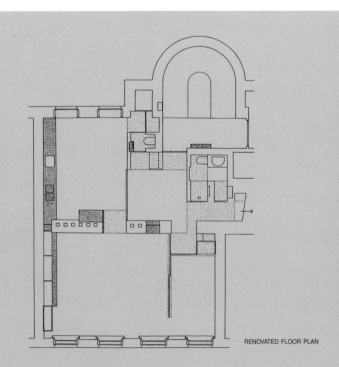

RENOVATED FLOOR PLAN

Concrete, metal, wood, and terrazzo are the materials chosen to configure the house's scale, therefore contrasting with the large white area. Metal is used for the profiles and the kitchen; the concrete plates as elements of scale transition; and the terrazzo in the bathrooms and for the kitchen-cooking top that continues toward the living room as shelves.

FINLAND **straw house**

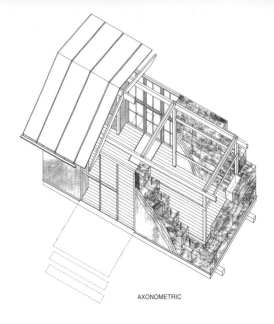

AXONOMETRIC

LOCATION	**Sattmark, Pargas, Finland**
SURFACE AREA	**150.64 sq. ft.**
ARCHITECT	**Jenni Reuter**
DATE	**1999**
PHOTOGRAPHERS	**Jenni Reuter / Juha Ilonen**

This unique cabin in a Finnish forest is located in a very appropriate environment for a building made with natural and recycled resources.

This small cabin was built with straw blocks over a wooden structure.

Materials were used that are very practical, economical, easy to acquire, with excellent qualities as acoustic and thermal insulation, ecological, pleasant, and energetically optimal.

Materials from the same area were employed to minimize transportation. The straw bales were obtained in the fields and dried during winter in a nearby barn. The wooden structure was collected from a forest in the area and even the surface foundation was made from uncut stone. Both the interior and exterior roughcast were made from local clay, sand, and straw.

A natural aspect of the straw bale construction is the maximum reduction of openings in the wall that is normally difficult to resolve technically. Therefore, the doors and windows were conceived as walls situated in the center of the longer sides.

There is room for four occupants in the interior, allowing for the installation of a simple kitchen, heater, and dining room table. There is a small wood porch projecting from the exterior for the summer time.

The cabin was created by amateur participants in a course on the construction of straw housing.

The good thermal state of this type of construction makes it appropriate to be installed in any environment; it can even be used during winter periods and hostile weather conditions.

The construction with straw bales follows the principles of conventional building. A main structure of wood beams and pillars supports the roof that resolves the evacuation of water. The holes are filled with 29.52 x 17.71 x 13.77 in. straw modules that are set up in the interior with wood bars. The bales have been roughcast with a mixture of clay, sand, and straw, and the unit was left unpainted to emphasize its basic and natural construction.

The built-up model can house up to four occupants. The architect proposed a few variations on the constructed prototype, typical of module-based architecture.

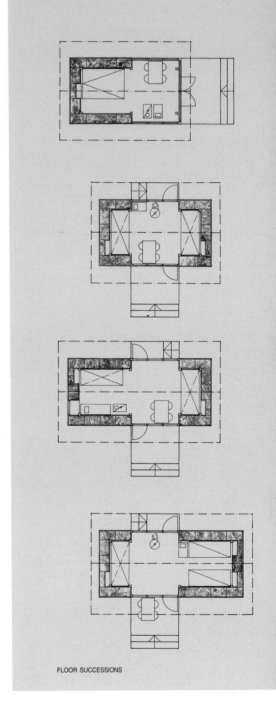

The windows, from an old mill, follow the ecological principle of recycling materials that is present in the entire design.

The difficulty of reinforcing the bending stress between straw modules drove the builders to create the windows like a panel between the straw walls, avoiding the presence of lintels.

FLOOR SUCCESSIONS

The cover or roof is supported with a structure of wood pillars, and the holes are filled with straw bales, just as in the construction, with a structure of concrete with brick enclosures.

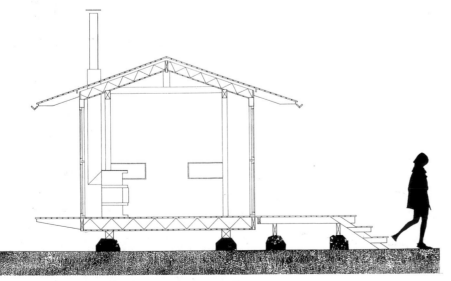

The straw bale construction is not anything new, but it has a great future due to the increase of wood prices and the large production of straw in the fields—a commercial solution to recycling and building more economical, comfortable, and ecological houses.

TOKYO seijo 6

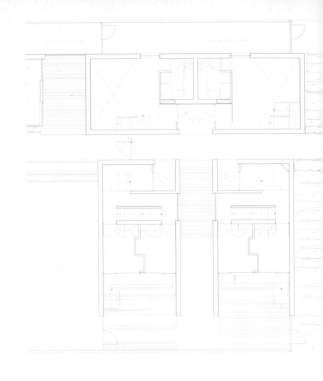

LOCATION **Tokyo, Japan**
SURFACE AREA **591.8 sq. ft.**
ARCHITECTS **Ken Yokogawa Architect & Associates Inc.**
DATE **2000**
PHOTOGRAPHER **Ryo Hata**

The building's exterior, built entirely in concrete, looks like a compact and massive volume where the light and luminous housing modules will be inserted afterward.

Located in an apartment complex made by the same architects, this dwelling completely reflects the characteristics that define the Japanese constructive spirit: economy of mediums, open distribution, and veracity of materials used. This apartment's deep patio, conceived as a pool of light that distributes and illuminates all the rooms, is fundamental in the design. Below the patio there is an area with a low roof that takes in the entrance and a kitchen that opens out into the living room. This area, resolved in two heights, has a large concrete wall down which the light from the patio trickles subtly. An elegant stairway with only one stringer extends the wood pavement toward the upper floor, where the bedroom, a dressing room area, and bathroom are located–adjacent to the pool of light.

All the rooms are visually connected to one another without the existence of conventional walls that split or divide the space. Even the bathroom has been separated from the bedroom by a glass parameter that maximizes the luminosity.

The light, controlled by the patio of light, trickles into all the apartment's corners, creating a subtle and elegant ambiance.

The materials used combine the wood for the pavement, the paint in white tones on the vertical parameters, and the visible concrete for the structural elements and the building's exterior.

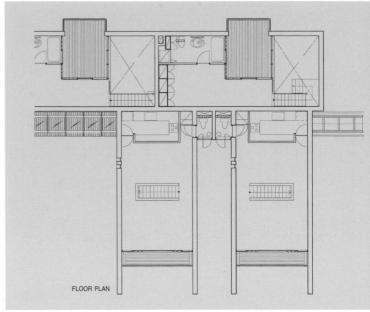

FLOOR PLAN

From the entrance, the large living room space is visible, and from there, the existence of an upper floor is sensed from the lofty stairway situated next to the wall. The light floods the entire space and is perceived as being very spacious due to the semidarkness that exists from this point of view.

The bathroom, adjacent to the bedroom, is enhanced by the views and the luminosity of a patio that also lights up the lower floor.

The wood pavement from the lower floor is also used on the stairway, integrating it into a space dominated by the modulated concrete wall that presides over the apartment's main room. The resulting room acquires an aspect of basic architecture, characteristic of Japanese design.

The materials were elegantly employed, combining the wood pavement with the wide concrete wall that dominates the apartment. The light from the patio trickles over the wall, granting a minimalist and elegant air to the space, typical of Japanese design.

CANTABRIA garage

LOCATION **Berría, Santoña, Spain**
SURFACE AREA **570.28 sq. ft.**
ARCHITECTS **Fernanda Solana Gabeiras**
Lorenzo Gil Guinea
Natalia Solana Gabeiras
DATE **2000**
PHOTOGRAPHER **Graphein**

The furniture module is the indisputable protagonist of this project. Its volumes fit in size and opening form to the spaces it serves.

The transformation of a garage into a multifunctional space was proposed (located on the lower ground floor of a house situated right on the beach) so that it could be used without distinction as a guest apartment, a place for family parties, or an extra space for certain daily activities of the family. For this, the owners suggested a plan with a kitchen, bedroom, bathroom, and living room.

The scarce light in the locale, with only the entrance and a high window as sources of light, the limited available height, and the situation of two central existing pillars, constitute the main determining factors of this project.

To develop this plan, a continuous floor was devised over which a furniture module was constructed to generate and serve the spaces that make up different elements of the plan. The location and dimensions of this were determined by the situation of the existing pillars that remain hidden, therefore achieving an open-plan space that is continuous with its surroundings. The other dividing element is the translucent glass–a characteristic that allows for maximum luminosity.

The furniture module was conceived as a smooth element stained purple with shiny varnish. The dark color makes it appear smaller, which makes the space appear larger; the glossy varnish lightens and de-emphasizes its presence, introducing light to the back of the apartment. With a solid appearance, it presents a quartering with different width joints that indicate the place and direction of the workable zones, whose openings are appropriate in size and form to the spaces that they will service.

A strategically situated multifunctional furniture unit organizes the whole apartment around it. The living room has been conceived as an open-plan space that is completely open to the exterior through hinged doors, allowing flexible use and configuring an ambiguous interior-exterior place.

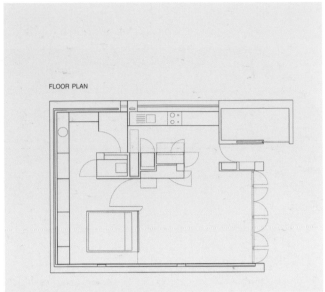

FLOOR PLAN

The varnish's shine contributes to a lighter feel and takes away from the massive presence of the furniture module, introducing light to the back of the apartment.

This project shows the storage space as a logically distributed element capable of conditioning and freeing all the space around it, giving rise to a continuous floor tinged with filters that visually or physically connect the entire space, therefore obtaining a flexibility of functions also for the owner.

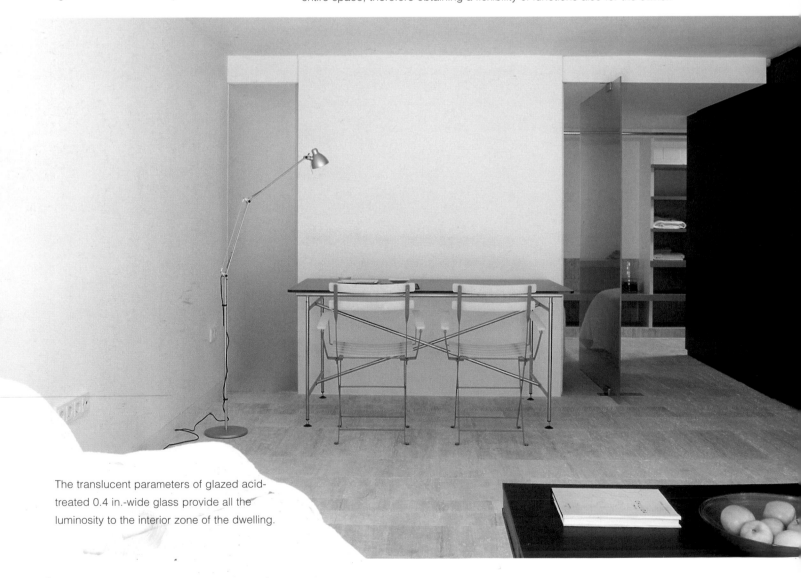

The translucent parameters of glazed acid-treated 0.4 in.-wide glass provide all the luminosity to the interior zone of the dwelling.

With a solid appearance, this piece of furniture presents
an irregular quartering of different-width sections that
indicate the place and direction of the practicable zones.

CROSS-SECTION

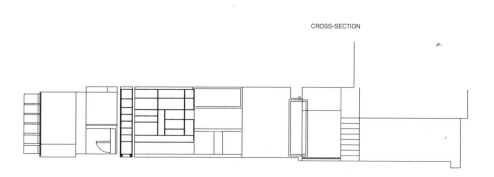

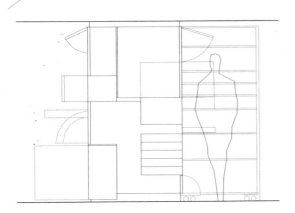

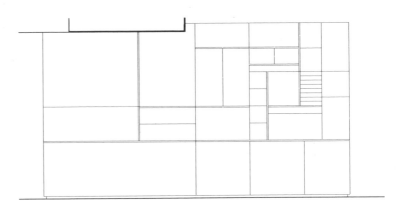

This proposal could only be made possible by the careful study of the furniture module's different sections and a suitable constructive rigor in its definition.

The kitchen is situated in direct relation to the living room. This perfectly allows for both more kitchen space for the upstairs dwelling as well as for outdoor parties.

The bathroom receives its light through the translucent glass that separates it from the kitchen. It is not understood as an independent space, rather as a fragment that interacts with the bedroom space.

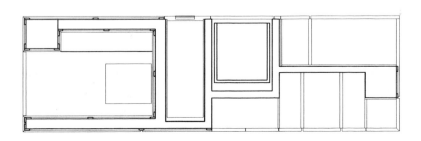

The bathroom is located among the shelves that occupy the wall at the back of the space.

The travertine serrated marble floor, with open pores 1.18 in. thick, provides a unitary character to the plan's spaces. This continuous floor accurately extends the vertical parameters, configuring a background for the bed, a base for the shelving, or a bench for resting in the bathroom.

Shelving was designed to cover the whole back of the apartment and extend into the bedroom and bathroom contributing to the two spaces being seen as unitary. This shelving adapts its function to each zone and serves successively as a closet, bench, and worktop.

The shower is made up of iroco wood boarding flush with the travertine floor on a gresite vessel for the drain. The toilet integrated into the furniture module is the bathroom's only element which remains visually separated from the rest.

ANYWHERE summer container

LOCATION anywhere
SURFACE AREA open 96.84 sq. ft.
closed 53.8 sq. ft.
ARCHITECT Markku Hedman
DATE 2000
PHOTOGRAPHER Markku Hedman

Growing ecological awareness and the current need to compress living spaces, emphasize the studio's necessity as a new minimum-sized living space that responds to the social and economic demand.

Finland's leafy forests housed the first model, where it perfectly blended in due to its construction and wood finishes.

This design consists of a wooden structure used for a vacation cabin that follows the principle of a matchbox.

It forms a hermetic cube for storage and transportation which is easily manipulated, and can be moved to the site by a trailer, or by dragging it as if it were a sled.

Once at the site, it can be opened out, and its volume doubles.

It has diverse functions: from a cabin for hikers to a mountain refuge to a vacation home for a young couple.

Its interior houses a kitchen, a desk, a space that can be used day and night, and a storage area. It can also be equipped with a kerosene burner and a heater, as well as a water tank and a sink. Solar panels or wind generators produce the electricity for this module.

All the parameters were made with different types of plywood boards covered in a phenolic resin. A thick polyester insulator was used as insulation between the boards, forming the prefabricated panels attached to the principal wood structure.

The unit forms a volume that reflects the colors of Finland's forests according to the different seasons.

Although this model is only a prototype, the current demand for transportable and economic housing can make it an ideal temporary residence.

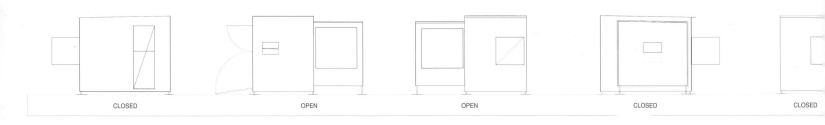

| CLOSED | OPEN | OPEN | CLOSED | CLOSED |

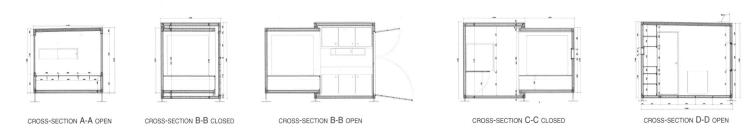

CROSS-SECTION A-A OPEN · CROSS-SECTION B-B CLOSED · CROSS-SECTION B-B OPEN · CROSS-SECTION C-C CLOSED · CROSS-SECTION D-D OPEN · CLOSED

The cube is only a prototype: it weighs 1543 lbs. although it
can weigh as little as 771 lbs. if produced in a series;
its estimated price is $ 8000; and its dimensions are
7.87 ft.-high, 8.18 ft.-wide, and 6.56 ft.-deep
when closed and 11.48 ft. when open.

All of its interior parameters, including the
flooring and the roofing, have been designed
in different tones of plywood, bringing
ecological awareness up to the last details.

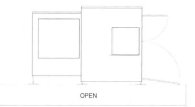

OPEN

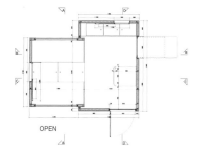

OPEN

When open, it looks like a more inviting element that benefits from the surrounding views. When closed, the unit looks hermetic, almost sculptural, and the wood panels that hide the interior seal off all openings.

The abstract conception and design allow this cabin module to be located anywhere; it can even be moved easily from one place to another given that it has self-sufficient energy resources.

MADRID loft in Barbieri

LOCATION	**Calle Barbieri, Madrid, Spain**
SURFACE AREA	**408.88 sq. ft.**
ARCHITECT	**Manuel Ocaña del Valle**
COLLABORATORS	**Celia López Aguado / Laura Rojo**
DATE	**2000**
PHOTOGRAPHER	**Luis Asin**

To maximize the dwelling's continuity, the space under the white staircase with wood steps and no rail is left free, allowing for an auxiliary closet. This, overall, forms a compact block.

What was previously a small space of hardly 408.88 sq. ft. under the cover of a 150-year-old building has been changed into a comfortable and modern apartment in the center of a large city. To increase the surface area, the 14.76 ft. height of the apartment (at the highest part) was divided into two floors, to maximize the space.

The plan for this renovation is extensive for an area with reduced available space, since the lower part includes a hall, living room, kitchen, bathroom, and terrace, and the upper part, the bedroom, bathroom, dressing room, and washing machine. In order to optimize the use of available space, it was necessary to make a rigorous study of the domestic scale that would stay away from traditional rigid models. For this, a strategy of flexible rooms was opted for, so that when the inhabitants want to eat, sit, or sleep, the entire space can be transformed into a dining room, living room, or bedroom.

This room is immersed in an urban neighborhood that is noisy and unorganized. The quest for peace and calmness at home requires a filter, a sound muffle, a transition space in between dwelling and city. This versatile and multipurpose space is a directional box of wood that relates the interior to the exterior.

A glazed closure relates the two parts, and the exterior rail is designed to also try to demarcate the dwelling's space by protecting it from the city.

The furniture is compact and integrated to form a part of the architecture. Therefore, under the stairs, there is a closet, and the kitchen and bathroom form a concentrated unit that allows the rest of the space to be free.

With an interest in creating an ambiance that transmits peace and quiet, the entire space is flooded with white, which, aside from providing a feeling of calmness, also enhances the idea of spaciousness. The white furniture also emphasizes this concept and is integrated in the architecture.

In the loft, the bathroom is separated from the bedroom by a parameter of translucent glass that provides the same spaciousness and visual continuity achieved in the rest of the apartment.

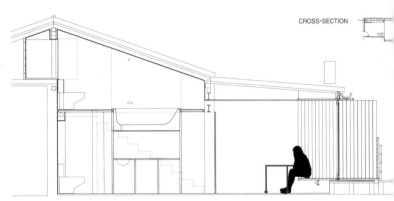

CROSS-SECTION

The detail of the bathtub, level with the upper floor and fitting in the center of the bathroom and kitchen, is an example of how the constructive technical aspect, rigor, and exactitude were determining elements to practically solve some of the construction's aspects.

The bathtub level with the floor is situated between the wall and a translucent parameter that suggests the space on the other side.

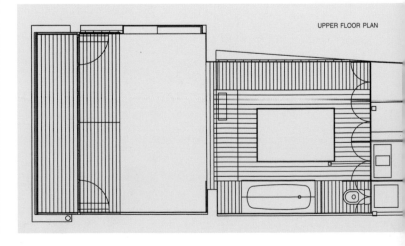

UPPER FLOOR PLAN

The terrace, elevated by wood and conceived to be like a filter between dwelling and city, extends the interior, giving rise to a protruding platform that can be used without distinction as a sofa or to form part of the exterior.

Thanks to the study of the domestic scale, and spatial maximizing avoiding conventional models, flexible rooms have been created that make this small apartment spacious.

The furniture designed exclusively for this apartment, especially this metallic table on wheels, grants the dining room spatial flexibility and multipurpose use.

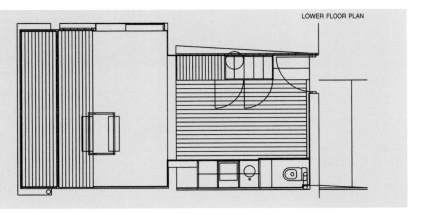

LOWER FLOOR PLAN

On the lower floor, the kitchen and staircase house the fixed storage zones, freeing the central space that extends to the exterior by the terrace wall. The furniture has been proposed as part of the architecture so that any residual space has been maximized.

A glazed closure divides the flexible wall of the terrace in two parts: the exterior railing also limits the apartment's space, protecting it from the city's noise.

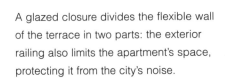

The kitchen, bathroom, and storage area are conceived as just one interrelated compact white block and the bathroom door slides in the kitchen, hiding part of it.

PARIS unique space

LOCATION **Rue Liancour, Paris, France**
SURFACE AREA **236.72 sq. ft.**
ARCHITECTS **Littow Architects**
DATE **2000**
PHOTOGRAPHER **J. Vasseur**

The owners of this pied-à-terre (small studio for occasional stays in Paris) organized the apartment in a rational manner, knocking down the old interior partitions. The furniture was also reduced as much as possible to avoid taking up too much the space.

An architect of the same nationality designed this apartment for a Finnish couple's temporary stays.

The apartment originally consisted of two rooms: a very old kitchen and bathroom.

From the beginning, the main objective was to reap the most benefits of the space, while avoiding a sense of suffocation. All the interior partitions were knocked down to achieve one large space that would benefit from facing two directions.

A wood podium was outfitted with shelves and drawers that could eventually accommodate a mattress and be converted into a bed.

The bathroom corner conceived to preserve the space's continuity was treated as lightly as possible with an enclosure of translucent glass.

There is mix of Finnish and French spirit in the materials used: Finnish birch plywood was used for the bed and bathroom's podium, as well as for the kitchen cupboards, and the other materials maintain the old characteristics of Paris. The original roble parquet and ceramic flooring bear witness to a touch of the old apartment's distribution.

This apartment, located on the top floor of a Parisian 14th arrondissement building, originally possessed two rooms. The living room and bedroom were made into one bright space due to the 236.72 sq. ft. of available space.

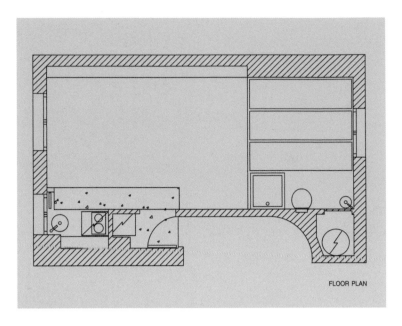

FLOOR PLAN

All of the corners in this apartment are pleasantly maximized. The block in the kitchen disappears into the space, also integrating the dwelling's entrance. The minimal but carefully distributed bathroom is absorbed in a corner of the wood podium, taking advantage of one of the old building's nooks to house the water heater.

Choosing materials and how to treat the space are voluntarily simple, almost aesthetic; space and light have been the top priority at all times.

A podium of Finnish birch plywood covered in four coats of polyurethane varnish creates the sleeping and bathing areas, storing some large drawers integrated in one element. Therefore, this platform can accommodate a mattress and eventually serve as a bed.

BARCELONA basic loft

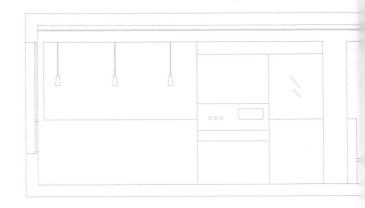

LOCATION	**Barcelona, Spain**
SURFACE AREA	**699.4 sq. ft.**
ARCHITECTS	**Anne Bugugnani / Diego Fortunato**
DATE	**2000**
PHOTOGRAPHER	**Eugeni Pons**

The clearly modulated large window that separates the apartment from the interior block patio, contributes a privileged luminosity shaded by white roller blinds.

The objective of this renovation was to convert a space that was previously used as a workshop–situated in an industrial rationalist building–into a studio apartment. The intrinsic qualities of the locale (an almost square space, with the floor plan and cross-section articulated by a central column and a transversal beam) and its natural light are taken advantage of. In spite of being located right in the urban center of Barcelona, in a zone with very busy streets and significant noise pollution, it has a privileged calmness, looking out onto the block's interior patio.

The restructuring program has distributed the apartment's essential functions in the space's perimeter to try to make the one room more versatile and to respect the natural light. The light comes from a chaotic-looking patio that contrasts with the order and calmness of the studio.

The studio is situated in the stairwell's fold. The open kitchen is built into a column under the transversal beam; the bathroom, shower, storage area, and bedroom are placed along a wall. The L-shaped dressing room forms the hall on one side, and on the other, a dining room area.

The kitchen, bathroom, and bedroom's volumes rise to the same height, a unit of 42.51 in., corresponding to the horizontal division of the large window.

The lighting is essential on this white stage. during the day, the stucco reflects all shades of the natural light's color, and at night, a few colored lamps hung with nylon string seem to be floating in space.

An eye-level opening in the corner
of the hall's parameter suggests
the space on the other side.

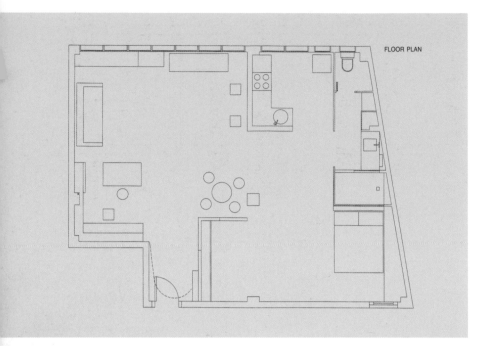

FLOOR PLAN

The functional spheres are placed, naturally, according to the characteristics of the available space. Therefore, the studio is situated in the stairwell's fold; the kitchen is built into a column under the transversal beam; and the bathroom, storage area, and bedroom are placed along a wall. The L-shaped dressing room forms a hall on one side, and on the other, a dining/living room area.

The plan was conceived in order to emphasize the contrast generated between the visual chaos of the interior patio–different architecture, clotheslines, and TV antennae–and the smoothness of the bright white stucco of all the study's interior parameters.

The corner of the building's stairwell has been taken advantage of to place the study, which also opens out to the central space.

The volumes that have been allocated the functions of kitchen, bathroom, and bedroom rise to the same height, a unit of 42.51 in., corresponding to the horizontal division of the large window. The shower's glass panels duplicate this height, as well as the dressing room, whose horizontal opening helps to emphasize the initial unit.

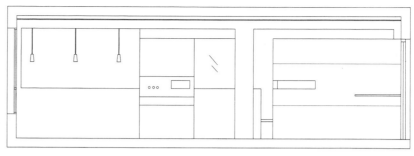

CROSS-SECTION

The clear and clean sculptural volume of the dressing room welcomes the hall: Because this zone does not reach the ceiling, it offers the visual continuity desired in the whole plan. A white curtain can be drawn in a curve, hiding the entrance to the apartment.

The bathroom, storage area, and bedroom have been arranged along the perimeter of a wall, opening up the central space, and receiving the natural light that comes from the patio. This emphasizes the unique way that the shower was devised, with a medium-high white perimeter and completely transparent glass around the upper part.

The white kitchen, under the transversal beam that orders the entire apartment, has been positioned between the area of activity and the bedroom area.

OSAKA atlas residence

LOCATION **Osaka, Japan**
SURFACE AREA **591.8 sq. ft.**
ARCHITECTS **Makoto Sei Watanabe**
ARCHITECTS' OFFICE
DATE **2000**
PHOTOGRAPHER **Makoto Sei Watanabe**

The architects tried to create an apartment complex that was the result of adding dwellings with different geometric forms unified by treating the exteriors in the same fashion. The result is a complex, a small city, where each of the group's dwellings maintains its own features and individuality.

The apartment complex located in an Osaka suburb serves as these Japanese architects' reflection about current and future collective housing. In a city where speculation is the law, a pleasant urbanization is imposed with the exterior space acting as the main element.

The geometric composition is not based on the juxtaposed addition of equal units, but rather on the integration of sixteen different housing geometries that are linked in order to make up a plaza with different routes, corners, and transitional spaces. In this manner the good work of the Japanese gardeners is extrapolated.

The houses are not joined by simply looking for a vertical volume; rather the architects try to integrate them into one recognizable block in the process of making the space's composition–but each module preserves its own individuality.

In accordance with the previous, the resulting complex is a live organism formed by different geometries combined to demarcate an interior space. For this, the design is not the result of a computer process (the most widely used method in current architecture), but rather a product of a humanized plan.

The color and texture unify the facades of the contrasting units that make up the complex. The floor and walls of the interior plaza are white, which accentuates the light and perspective of the space. Narrow windows of different proportions and gold-colored borders reflect the sunlight that unifies the architectural complex.

The entrances to the houses are made of different paths and bridges that incorporate the principle of flexibility and diversity of uses pertaining to the conception of a city formed by heterogeneous principles.

The apartment's floor plan, just like the urbanization, shows it as an organism of identifiable parts that make up a whole. A compact block contains the essential areas for a house: access, bedrooms, bathrooms, and storage areas. At the same time, each of this block's units can be broken down in smaller parts that enrich and give life to the apartment. All of this concentrated distribution comes out into the organism's head: a circular room with an open kitchen.

The wood and the light that come from the impressive view of the large cylindrical room, where the complex's interior patio is made out, gives the interior a comfortable feel.

The wood was used for the walls and the floor to achieve a clean and welcoming space. For its spaciousness and shape, it constitutes a room of diverse uses: a room for parties, a space for resting, or simply a viewpoint where the entire apartment complex can be made out.

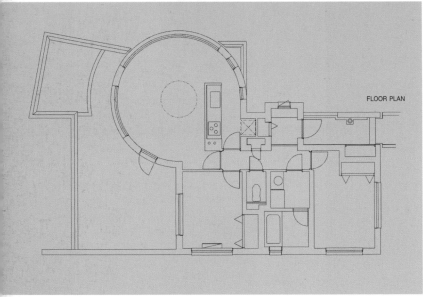

FLOOR PLAN

The composition of this apartment can be differentiated into two zones: one is formed by the homogenous group of typical rooms, and the other by a unique open-plan cylindrical room. The apartment is accessed by a broken distribution that links juxtaposed rooms: two bedrooms and a bathroom block. This on the whole flows into a large room that is open to the complex's interior plaza and includes, as the only transgressor element of this clear space, a kitchen that is also open and acts to unify with the rest of the apartment.

The relation between the interior and exterior, looked for in the urbanization's entire design, is the most expressive in this clear view with a terrace that literally hovers over the complex's interior plaza.

The circular form, based on basic architecture, is not often used in current apartment buildings due to its constructive complexity. However it is the ideal structure for an interior space–because there are no edges, there are no residual spaces.

PALMA carrer llums

LOCATION	**Carrer Llums, Palma de Mallorca, Spain**
SURFACE AREA	**559.52 sq. ft.**
ARCHITECT	**José M. Pascual Cañellas**
DATE	**2001**
PHOTOGRAPHER	**Santiago Garcés**

A very complete apartment has been obtained from a floor plan with square proportions in both its distribution of space and furniture and fittings.

Access is gained by a small staircase that forms a part of the apartment, then flows into a spacious living room, capable of housing different spaces.

A fully equipped kitchen opens out to the living room, separated from the main space by a translucent partition. This optically opens up the living room area and creates a space where the shadows of utensils used daily are projected.

In a separate space, the house's most private areas are located and distributed by a small hall: bedroom, dressing room, and bathroom. The bathroom has generous but contained dimensions that are optimally distributed into two spaces, so that two or more people can use them simultaneously. There is an area for the bath and sink and another area separated by a sliding door–to gain space–which accommodates the toilet, bidet, and shower.

The entire apartment was painted white to highlight the luminosity on a roble-covered floor. The furniture and decoration correspond perfectly to a modern and rational environment.

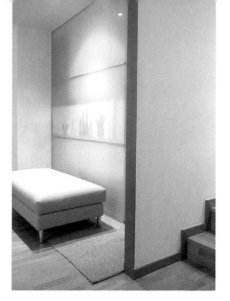

A translucent screen that separates the living room suggests, through projected shadows, the blue-toned kitchen fittings. Also, this solution brings certain luminosity to the interior kitchen.

The fairly spacious living room is made up of two different spaces: one for daily use, equipped with current furniture, and another more relaxed space, next to a large bookcase, where the inhabitant can rest lying down in a beautiful chaise-lounge.

The kitchen, with an excellent U-shaped layout, takes advantage of the parameters for storage.

A granite green is used for the kitchen fittings combined with blue-toned closets.

The most effective distribution for a floor plan with square proportions was chosen for this apartment. The entrance, situated in the center, flows out onto a small staircase that leads to a spacious living room and visually joined to a large kitchen. The bedroom, dressing room, and bathroom areas are located in a separate area, forming an independent and private unit.

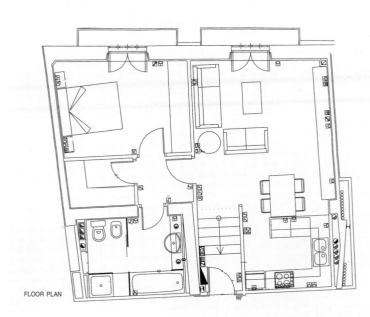

FLOOR PLAN

To obtain a smaller and functional space, the bathroom was divided into two spaces: the sink and bath are located in one of them, and in the other, the shower, toilet, and bidet.

SYDNEY the grid

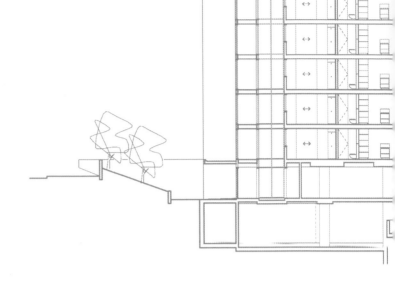

LOCATION	**Bayswater Road Rushcutters Bay, Sydney, Australia**
SURFACE AREA	**548.76 sq. ft.**
ARCHITECT	**Engelen Moore**
DATE	**2001**
PHOTOGRAPHER	**Ros Honeysett**

This apartment forms part of an apartment block called The Grid in Sydney, Australia. This block includes housing with one, two, and three bedrooms.

A prestressed concrete structure creates markedly longitudinal boxes where the housing is located. All the apartments are organized in the same fashion: interior center which accommodates the kitchen, bathroom, and storage areas; the bedrooms, located in the interior section of the building; and the living room in the exterior section, with an open kitchen and a large terrace.

The same flooring is found in all the rooms and the white-toned plaster on the vertical parameters constitutes the unity of the entire plan. The treatment of the panels in different colors, used for doors and closets, achieves a large chromatic diversity that distinguishes each apartment.

There is track lighting that allows for groups of lights to be placed in the areas with the most activity at any moment–this clearly responds to a continuous housing design that is personalized by each owner.

The apartment block, called The Grid, clearly alluding to its cell-based structure, is a display of the latest prolific generation of Australian architects.

The apartments are accessed through an elegant glass corridor with two large pools of light that, adjacent to the interior bedrooms, offer them lighting and privacy.

The main space is a clear, sculptural, open-plan box in which the kitchen opens out onto the living room–it has very lively colored panels, specifically chosen for each apartment. The zenithal track lighting offers the owner the possibility of situating the lights in accordance with their function at each time of day.

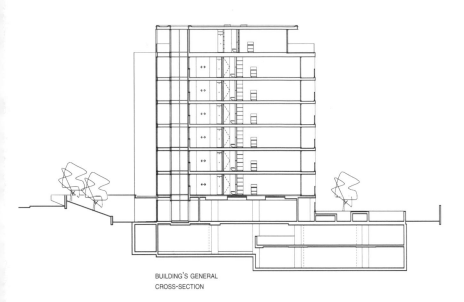

BUILDING'S GENERAL
CROSS-SECTION

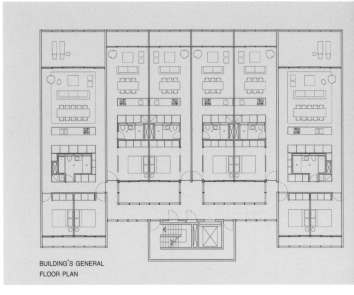

BUILDING'S GENERAL
FLOOR PLAN

All the apartments, whether one, two, or three bedrooms, are organized in the same fashion: a longitudinal plan with natural ventilation at both of the apartment's extremes, and a center that separates the bedrooms from an open-plan living room that extends into a terrace.

The chromatic variety and personalization of the wood panels in each apartment offers each owner a unique characteristic within the block's collectivity.

A large sliding door reaching from the floor to the ceiling separates the bedroom from the corridor, but because it doesn't occupy the entire length, offers visual relief to the entrance hall.

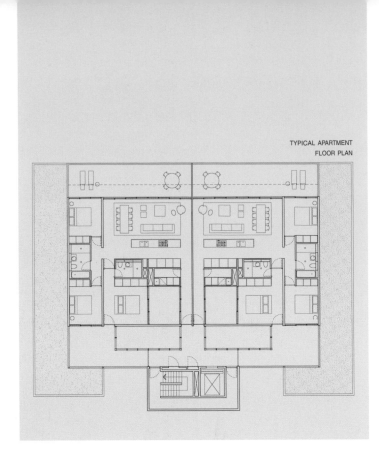

TYPICAL APARTMENT
FLOOR PLAN

A longitudinal corridor determines all the rooms. At the entrance it merges with the bedroom, and at the end it opens out into an open-plan space that pours out onto a spacious terrace.

The design mechanism is the same for the one-bedroom apartments as for the larger apartments: the central area as the apartment's heart, and a large open-plan room with subtle lighting.

All the apartment's terraces project out toward an exterior area with gardens and a large pool.

The design lends itself to the use of contemporary criteria for its furnishing. But the architect offers only a modern background where each owner can later furnish the apartment in accordance to his/her taste.

NEW YORK sjoberg residence

LOCATION **New York City, New York, United States**

SURFACE AREA **559.52 sq. ft.**

ARCHITECT **Abigail Shachat, AJS Design/s**

DATE **2001**

PHOTOGRAPHER **Bjorg**

From the access area, separated by a light steel railing, the living room, with an incorporated fireplace, dominates. The furnishings were selected to suit a comfortable and relaxed environment. The bedroom, separated by a partition, does not lose its permeability because it is linked to the exterior by a window on the upper floor.

The young thirty-year-old professional who owns this apartment wanted to obtain a contemporary space that would reflect his personal lifestyle in his first apartment.

Aided by a total height of almost 16.40 ft., this unique apartment is developed into three floors, all of which are visually related. The middle floor that provides access to the kitchen and dining room also incorporates a bathroom. The living room area is located on the lower floor, and the upper floor is made up of the bedroom, bathroom, and dressing room. All of these areas are connected and form a whole in which the rooms can be perceived from any point. From the access, the living room, bedroom, and kitchen can be made out with a glance. At the same time, the hall and living room area can be seen from the kitchen on the lower floor and visitors can be seen at the apartment's entrance from a wide window in the bedroom.

The two flights of stairs unite all the rooms, emphasizing the sense of connection and vertical movement. With a unique design, this stairway constitutes a point of union between the different areas.

The furniture adds a second layer to the architecture, chosen for its comfort, simplicity, and for not obstructing vision from any point—a generating element of the design.

The meticulous details of the furnishings and complements dot all of the rooms. The furniture combines functionality with a pleasant and elegant design.

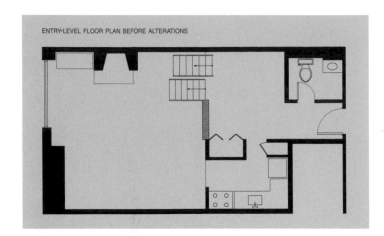

ENTRY-LEVEL FLOOR PLAN BEFORE ALTERATIONS

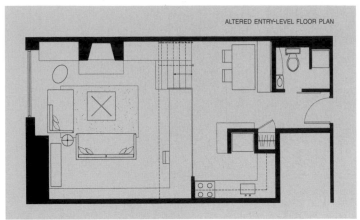

ALTERED ENTRY-LEVEL FLOOR PLAN

The alteration of this apartment was made subtly through the elimination of elements such as partitions and closets; therefore obtaining one space fragmented in three heights. The entry level, formed by the bathroom and kitchen, was separated from the lower living room by a light railing, leaving the whole space integrated.

Under the kitchen, making the most of the recess of the upper floor's volume, a studio table is placed longitudinally in front of the living room from where the kitchen can also be made out.

The two flights of stairs, as the apartment's main feature, were designed with pieces of wood that show how it connects the rooms. The way it is dealt with also relates to how the rooms are united: massive on the lower part for the apartment's public area and lofty on the upper part like a bridge of union to the bedroom–the most private room of the apartment.

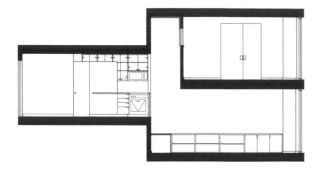

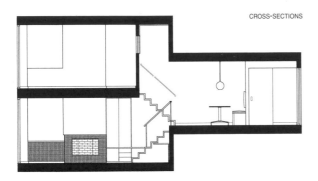

CROSS-SECTIONS

The bathroom was made with great aesthetic skill, selecting indircct lighting and elegant and functional bathroom fittings.

The cross-section is the best representation for perceiving a space with these characteristics. In this, the bedroom block, situated on the upper floor, is set in place in respect to the entry-level floor to visually increase the space and take in the nucleus of the stairway.

In the kitchen, located in the corner, there are two areas: one visible from the access and the living room, and another more protected area for preparing food.

The wall-to-wall carpet and the treatment of the windows and closets favor the feel of a secluded and relaxed environment, contrasting with the spaciousness of the other rooms.

A face of windows that offers both permeability and privacy visually connects the upper floor, which takes in the most private area of the bedroom and dressing room.

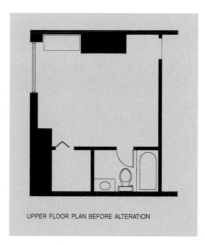

UPPER FLOOR PLAN BEFORE ALTERATION

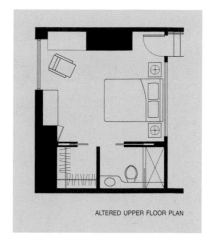

ALTERED UPPER FLOOR PLAN

There is a wide window without woodwork above the bed that offers a vision of the entry area. Sliding panels that make the area more spacious substituted the doors to the dressing room and bathroom.

BARCELONA **poble nou**

<table>
<tr><td>LOCATION</td><td>**Barcelona, Spain**</td></tr>
<tr><td>SURFACE AREA</td><td>**516.48 sq. ft.**</td></tr>
<tr><td>ARCHITECTS</td><td>**Sandra Aparicio**
Ignacio Forteza</td></tr>
<tr><td>DATE</td><td>**2001**</td></tr>
<tr><td>PHOTOGRAPHER</td><td>**Santiago Garcés**</td></tr>
</table>

The living room offers a complete view of the entire apartment. The kitchen, located next to the entrance, opens out onto this luminous room, which also connects to the upper floor where the most private area of the apartment is situated. The two floors of this room and the luminosity of the large frontal area of windows helps to visually enlarge the entire space.

Starting with a floor plan in the shape of a box, hardly 430.55 sq. ft., favored by its 14.76 ft.-height, a minimal plan was created which developed two heights for a couple. The obtained result is a spacious open-plan space, immersed in a neutral and luminous atmosphere.

The kitchen, dining room, and living room are situated on the lower floor. From there, a metal ladder provides access to the upper floor where the bedroom and bathroom are accommodated. Both upper and lower spaces remain visually connected. A stainless steel counter for the kitchen accompanies the apartment's entrance. Behind this, a block of tall, white Formica closets store the electrical appliances and a pantry, also hiding a drawer where the building's installations pass. At the end of the kitchen, the metallic carpentry with aluminum strips, allows for natural light to enter into the apartment.

The ladder, with 0.39 in. painted white iron sheets, was placed parallel to the dividing wall. Some DM wood shelves accompany this ladder; they are lacquered in white up to the main concrete beam that was left visible. The living room is located in the double space, with a sofa, an armchair, a few extra tables, and two bookshelves below the large window standing out. The furniture is all in light-toned wood to contrast with the darker floor, offering luminosity to the room.

When going up the ladder, the railing ends in the form of a table, accommodating a studio area lit up by a square practicable skylight. This L-shaped table changes function in the bedroom's passing-by area, where a bathroom sink is located. There is a large mirror above this sink that seemingly doubles the space and, in front of it, a sliding door that closes off the shower and toilet area.

Then, a niche in the wall that separates the bathroom holds a simple wardrobe with metal bars, leading to the bedroom.

Between the dividing wall and the ladder, there is an elegant and plentiful set of shelves also built in white. The color, reflected here on the books, will be a product of use and the passing of time.

The same elements throughout the apartment are repeated in the bedroom: a room in white tones, a main beam of concrete seen over the bed, and a line of windows at the back of the room, giving the entire space a neutral and harmonious atmosphere.

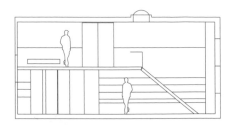

The development of two heights, an underlying element of modern architecture, unfolds with great style and care in this apartment, which in spite of its limited space becomes a luxury apartment and demonstrates the architect's ability to make the most of a small area.

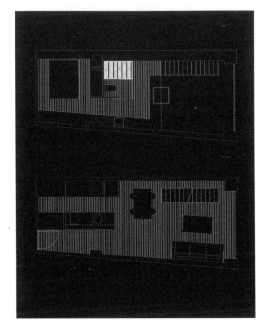

In a narrow space of hardly 13.12 sq. ft., the architects opted for a more rational and practical design: the kitchen situated next the entrance, opens out into the living room; a ladder in line with the kitchen frees the rest of the space to make up the apartments main room. On the upper floor, the closed shower and toilet form a block that separates the bedroom's study area.

Due to its limited space, the living room area was strategically furnished to not provoke a feeling of suffocation. All the free parameters were taken advantage of to house shelves where books can be placed.

Due to the living room's double height, the view from the upper floor offers a splendid panoramic of a spacious and large space, therefore creating a continuous apartment, in both its conception and use.

The elegant combination of materials like the steel and white lacquered wood for the kitchen show the careful gusto for detail that the authors inspired in the entire design.

The loft railing was transformed into a desk that projects from the living room's upper area. Made from dark, dyed okume wood, it changes its use in the bedroom's passing-by area, housing a sink in front of the shower and toilet.

The shower is protected by a large partition of translucent butiral glass with woodwork in stainless steel, that allows for natural light to enter. The bath was covered in sand-colored ceramic pieces, leaving the main concrete beam visible that appears in all of the apartment's rooms. The bath dais is made of teka, and the faucets are by designer Phillippe Stark.

The suppression of the doors that separate the different rooms, helped by the continuity of the furniture, provokes a sensation of a continuous and fluid space that the entire design aims for. However, the necessary demarcation for the privacy of the bedroom is made with the large compact block that holds the bathroom–visually linking the two rooms.

PARIS petits champs

LOCATION	**Rue des Petits Champs, Paris, France**
SURFACE AREA	**387.36 sq. ft.**
ARCHITECT	**Philippe Challes**
DATE	**2001**
PHOTOGRAPHER	**Patrick Müller**

The design began with an open-plan floor without any interior partition or functional spaces like a kitchen or bathroom. The adopted strategy consisted of dividing the apartment in two parts corresponding to the apartment's uses and making the most of the existing geometry: on one hand, a spacious room with an incorporated kitchen for use as a living room in the day and a bedroom at night, and on the other hand, a storage area, dressing room, and bathroom independent from the main space.

This sixth-floor apartment, in Paris's 1st arrondissement, benefits from a large amount of light.

Before being renovated, it was a 365.97-sq. ft. open-plan floor without a bathroom, kitchen, and with scarce storage areas.

The owner wanted to benefit from the most spacious surface area possible, without invading the space with furniture and other types of elements. The owner also wanted a kitchen and a bathroom with reasonable dimensions integrated into the space.

To respect all these interests, the renovation began by extending the apartment by 21.52 sq. ft., taking space from the common access area. The entrance was placed in front of the windows next to a deep closet. All the common spaces are lined up along a wall, and the L-shaped kitchen presides over the 252.95-sq. ft. living room/bedroom lit by two large windows.

A dressing room and closet area are situated behind the kitchen; also serving as a link between the main space and the dwelling's most private area, the bathroom.

The overall design is minimalist in both the treatment of the spaces and in the use of materials. The living room/bedroom was painted in white matte and the kitchen furniture and entrance closet are made of polished aluminum.

Thanks to the two large windows, situated in the inclined walls–typical of the upper floors in Haussman style buildings–this small studio is very spacious.

The owner wanted the largest surface area possible, without invading the space with elements that would limit it. For this reason, the kitchen was integrated into one of the living room's main walls, freeing up the rest of the apartment's space.

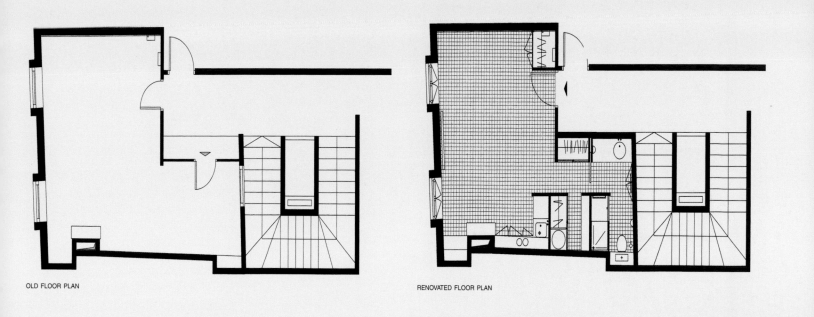

OLD FLOOR PLAN

RENOVATED FLOOR PLAN

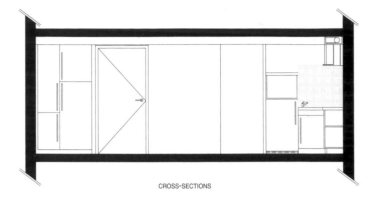

CROSS-SECTIONS

The fixed storage elements like the kitchen, dressing room, and closets were carefully studied in their quartering because they are the most important design elements in this apartment.

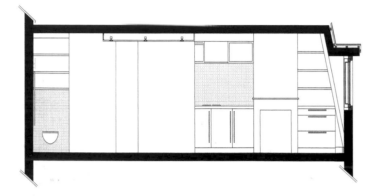

The kitchen presides over the main living room/bedroom space. The modern and functional kitchen fittings are made with aluminum and stainless steel for the cooking top.
All of the apartment's corners were maximized; the existing space on both sides of the chimney was used to place the kitchen and the custom-made shelves.

A hallway from the house's main area distributes the most personal spaces: closet, dressing room, and bathroom. Its 31.50 in. width is limited, but this seems alleviated by the dressing-room space with no physical limit by the hallway, and with the use of sliding doors on the closets and the bathroom.

From the main space, you can sense the presence of other more private rooms within the dwelling. When the door that separates both zones is left open, the apartment's very small space is visually magnified.

The bathroom area, which is accessed by a sliding door, is made the most of and divided into two areas: the gresite sink area with a mirror that occupies the entire parameter, and the more private shower and toilet area, which invades the apartment's last corner.

MILAN malta apartment

LOCATION **Milan, Italy**
SURFACE AREA **505.71 sq. ft.**
ARCHITECT **Ignacio Cardenal**
DATE **2001**
PHOTOGRAPHER **Santiago Garcés**

Crossed and open views of the rest of the rooms are available from any point in the apartment. The clean and modern furniture is used as an element to separate the rooms, therefore avoiding unnecessary conventional partitions.

In this apartment, based on the spatial and visual continuity between the different rooms, the existing ceiling is taken advantage of to create an open-plan two-level space.

A loft was created with visible metallic sheets under the vaulted framework, and a bedroom was placed there that is completely open to the lower space and adjacent to a spacious dressing room and a room set aside as a library and studio.

Below this original platform, a living room, dining room, kitchen, and an original bathroom are located; the latter is separated by a translucent paved partition.

The modern and current materials contrast with the old building of visible brick, making it look like an industrial loft. Special attention was also paid to the furniture so that it would act to separate the different rooms, therefore avoiding the traditional partitions that only restrict the space.

The result is a continuous volume that is spacious and luminous, where all the apartment's rooms can be made out from any point–making this hardly 500 sq. ft. room a spacious and cozy space.

A small hallway that shows the design's key materials forms the entrance. An original wall of visible brick will be supported by the white painted parameters.

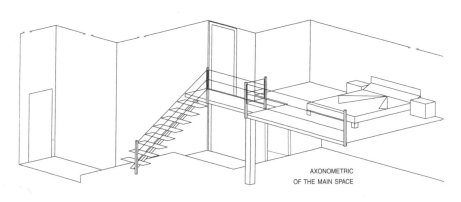

AXONOMETRIC
OF THE MAIN SPACE

The metal platform that accommodates the bedroom is the design's main feature. All of the lower and peripheral space accepts this ethereal and lofty platform.

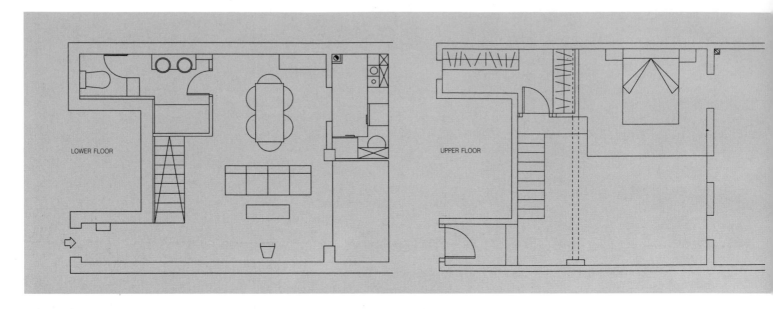

LOWER FLOOR

UPPER FLOOR

Due to the limited available surface area, the architect tried to maintain a clean and open geometry without breaking it with unnecessary interior partitions. For this, the loft that accommodates the bedroom was placed in the center of the apartment, opening out over the main space, and around it the different closed rooms are distributed, including the dressing room, studio zone, kitchen, and bathroom.

The space under the bedroom's platform was used to place the bathroom and a dining room separated simply from the main space by a sofa.

The materials and careful lighting offer an affable and warm vision of this continuous, fluid, and open space.

NEW YORK wilkinson mini-loft

LOCATION	**Greenwich Village, New York City, New York, United States**
SURFACE AREA	**505.71 sq. ft.**
ARCHITECT	**Andrew Wilkinson**
DATE	**2001**
PHOTOGRAPHER	**James Shanks**

The living room, which offers a complete view of this mini-loft, is spatially joined to the kitchen. Above them, taking advantage of the apartment's height, a narrow stairway leads to the apartment's upper part, where a large bedroom is located.

The apartment only has three windows that look to the outside, and one of them offers an impressive view of the Empire State Building.

When Andrew Wilkinson, a Manhattan architect who recently opened his own studio, acquired this apartment, he saw the possibility to increase its surface area by installing a second floor to accommodate a large bedroom.

The apartment, with rectangular proportions, was developed along a longitudinal hall that accesses the bathroom and the storage areas, and flows into a kitchen that opens out into the living room. You can reach the bedroom that opens over the living room by a narrow staircase adjacent to the wall; in the bedroom there is a king-size bed and a desk that projects over the lower space. In this manner, all the spaces converge toward the living room, the only exterior space, which also offers an impressive view of the Empire State Building.

Keeping in mind the necessity for storage space, special care was taken in the treatment of the closets–both with the existing ones and the new ones. The old closets were too narrow and were renovated, increasing their lower back area to hang clothes, maintaining the upper area for the folded clothing–therefore forming a functional unit with minimum visual impact. Also, the stairway that provides access to the upper floor was formed with superimposed wooden boxes to hold different objects and elements in their interior.

The materials used combine the wood in the pavement, the light tones of the parameters, and a gray-blue color for the new floor's structures. The view of the structure and the chromatics of the upper framework have been maintained, offering an industrial air to the space that is typical of North American lofts.

CROSS-SECTION

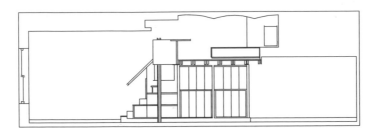

The cross-section allows the apartment's four main spaces to be seen: an initial hall, a closet area in front of the kitchen, and a main space, linked to the bedroom.

By inserting an extra leaf, the dining room table can expand to seat four diners. This resource is part of almost all modern tables due to limited space.

The kitchen, situated between the bathroom and living room, was understood as an element that could create more spaciousness; therefore, it was created to open out onto the living room. An island of furniture, which also acts to give more space to the dining room table, separates the kitchen and living room.

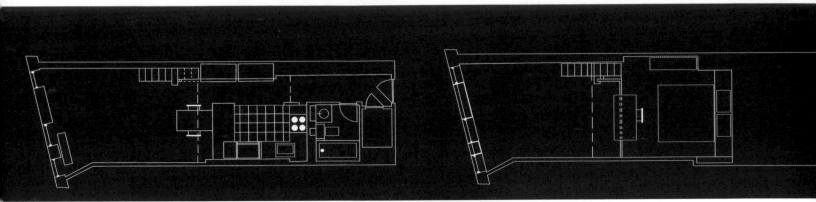

The floor plan was created to try to counteract the excessive back of the apartment, trying to decrease the hall's longitude as much as possible. For this reason, the hallway–which only distributes toward the bathroom and a small walk-in closet–is expanded into the kitchen that opens out on the living room, therefore obtaining a spacious main area. This space is also reinforced by the visual continuity established between the lower floor and the bedroom.

Special care was taken in the renovation of the apartment's closets, obtaining more functional elements that do not visually alter the design.

The staircase, inspired by the architect's business trip to Japan, represents a unique element of the apartment. Its composition is based on simple wooden planks that form cubicles, allowing for the storage of household equipment in their interior.

The bathroom, austere but functional, combines ceramic and wooden bathroom furnishings. The lighting design, present in the whole apartment, is also considered here with the insertion of a luminous box in the mirrored furnishing.

The bedroom plays with two concepts common to the entire design: comfort and practicality. Comfort is represented by the king-size bed, practicality by the large amount of closets and shelves.

MEXICO CITY chimali

LOCATION	**Chimalistac, Mexico City, Mexico**
SURFACE AREA	**430.4 sq. ft.**
ARCHITECTS	**Gumà Arquitectes**
DATE	**2001**
PHOTOGRAPHER	**Santiago Garcés**

This small and elegant apartment is a distinguished and refined space that is pleasantly maximized.

Its interior layout is simple and clear: a hallway that distributes toward the bedroom, kitchen, and the main dining room area, and an area for reflection and relaxing. Aside from this simple distribution, the care taken for the treatment of the space and light make it a perfect example of making the most of a space and being meticulous with the details.

The elegantly furnished main room, set aside for the living room, is conceived as an open-plan space. In the center of this room, in front of a window made from u-glass–a modern and current symbol of the contemporary element that prevails in the design–there is a table that can be used as a desk or a table for eating. In front of the table, there is a folding wood screen that can act as a changeable element to separate a room and there is also a small enclosure set in a closet, which can be used as a unique area for relaxation of even as an improvised bedroom.

The whole space created is a limited one where the preciosity of the materials and the care taken with the light are what prevail in the design.

A small table and shelf are set in the hallway to allow for this space to be used as a study area. The necessary diffused lighting is subtly provided through an opening over the bedroom volume.

An elegant light-wood folding screen acts as a separating element for the two rooms. Its curved geometry also is related to the room's furniture.

An original table flanked by two modernist chairs is placed in the middle of the space. The lighting of this table is this room's main feature; the window it leans against provides an unusual luminosity and clarity over it that reflects onto the entire room. A zenithal opening from a hole in the ceiling also increases the dominating luminous characteristic of this area in the space.

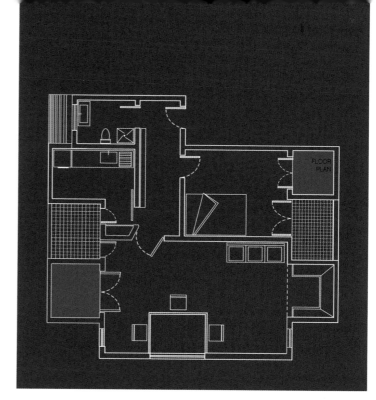

FLOOR PLAN

The elegant furniture used mixes straight and modern lines with curvaceous elements. The contemporary armchair blends with colorist pleasant chairs. And the curved elements are formalized by the distinguished folding screen and a carpet that introduces a fun note into the design.

VIENNA box-studio

LOCATION **Vienna, Austria**
SURFACE AREA **538 sq. ft.**
ARCHITECTS **lichtblau . wagner architekten & Associates Inc.**
DATE **2002**
PHOTOGRAPHER **Bruno Klomfar**

The alteration of this apartment forms part of a group of four studios located in the attic. All of them lead out into a nucleus of open stairs above the apartment's entrance. The entrance, simple yet direct, breaks with those of conventional apartments by directly accessing a large hall from the stairs, collected by the volume of the box-studio situated in the upper area.

The restructuring of this attic is characterized by simplifying ideas adapted to the field of architecture. While in residential and conventional designs, the main preoccupation lies in functional or aesthetic aspects, and these architects based this work on economizing energy, money, and space.

Due to the limitation of available surface area, the design offers flexibility of utilities through the elimination of circulation areas. The different uses are linked together, avoiding the conventional space dedicated to the hallway. Therefore, all the rooms are distributed to the sides of a border where the bathroom and kitchen areas are located. In this manner, the distribution and utilities are open, allowing the function of the space to be changed according to the time of day.

A unique element has been inserted into the apartment that seems to float in space: a compact capsule for the workroom or rest area. This can be accessed by a mobile stair/closet filled with different storage compartments, which when moved can change the morphology of the surrounding space. The texture and uniqueness constitute a differential element of these architects' work.

The materials used are simple but very good. The vertical concrete parameters are left visible over the continuous wood pavement, therefore minimizing the cost of intervention. A yellow box stands out on the parameters, topping off a daring project.

Inside, the idea of the capsule was taken to an extreme and its walls and ceilings were built in the same yellow tone as the exterior, and the stairs drilled into the floor. This increases the feeling of the one space placed on top of the concrete structure.

The yellow capsule is the design's most unique element. Its form and texture are a counterpoint to the harsh concrete architecture used for the vertical parameters. As well as acting as a work or rest area, its stairs can be opened by a simple mechanism to collect the household equipment that is stored inside–changing the morphology of the adjacent space.

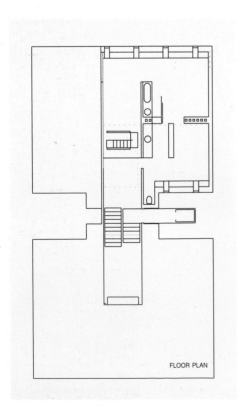

FLOOR PLAN

From an entrance protected by the upper volume of the box-studio, three adjacent rooms are accessed that are not demarcated in advance for established uses. In the center of all of them, like a generating axis, the humid zones of the bathroom and kitchen open toward the adjacent space. As far as its possible uses, this on the whole forms one modern space with many compartments.

NEW YORK echart-baldwin residence

LOCATION **New York, United States**
SURFACE AREA **699.4 sq. ft.**
ARCHITECTS **DZO Architecture**
Arnaud Descombes / Elena Fernandez
Antoine Regnault / David Serero
DATE **2002**
PHOTOGRAPHER **Anne-Sophie Restoux**

Located in an apartment block close to the former World Trade Center, this apartment was altered using materials and atmosphere to create a pleasant and open space. The design plays with the mobility of the surfaces and the interior furnishing as a way to reconfigure a living space, granting it a wide versatility of uses.

Swinging and sliding panels of different materials divide or filter the spaces, visually altering the spatial limits.

A small hallway that pours out into the living room is the apartment's entrance. There are a few elegant and exclusive birch wood cabinets-shelves hung from the wall to store household equipment, hide audio and video equipment, and disguise the air conditioning unit. In front of the windows, these cabinet-shelves turn into a bench, creating a wonderful viewpoint over the city.

A large panel of green glass opens the bedroom toward the main space, creating a totally open space in an apartment with great physical and visual limitations.

The kitchen, built entirely of wood, was conceived as an independent container, facing the main living room space. Lit on its perimeter, it seems to float over the main space.

With similar resources, the lighting and location of the speakers inlaid in the roof develop the background atmosphere desired at each moment or according to the mood. Therefore, the house can be decorated for different atmospheres: musical, romantic, Zen, or festive.

Two main spaces in the floor plan are joined in a refined way: a living room where the kitchen container opens toward the space, and a bedroom with a bathroom and dressing room. Both are joined by an interstitial space that, separated by an elegant translucent glass sliding door, can be transformed into a more spacious living room.

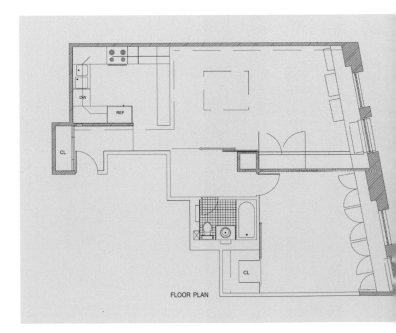

FLOOR PLAN

The materials used mix the wood for the pavement, kitchen, and closet with a treatment in light tones used on the vertical parameters. By limiting the number of materials, the space is unified.

An elegant element formed by cabinets hung on the wall with swinging doors, and a lower bench go around the apartment's perimeter. When meeting the face of windows, on the whole it becomes an intentional viewpoint over the city's skyline.

The quartering and arrangement of the different cabinets and shelves were carefully studied to create a useful area that made the most of a limited space.

The care taken with the materials and the study of the constructive details are displayed here in the subtle union of the set of shelves-cabinets with swinging doors.

The lighting, superimposed on the architecture, creates a feeling of warmth, emphasizing the different elements of the house. Therefore, the kitchen, with a subtly illuminated perimeter, is visually demarcated, and seems to float in the space.

A sliding translucent green glass panel makes the transition from the living room toward the bedroom area. Its transparency and lightness break down the two areas, contributing to the apartment's visual unity.

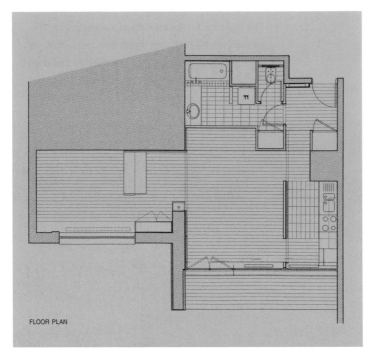

From a small hallway protected by closets,
a fully equipped bathroom can be accessed.
The kitchen, aligned with the hallway, is separated
from the living room by a partition wall with two
sliding doors—these visually clear out the space.
The bedroom is separated from the living room
by a large sliding door, which allows the entire
apartment to be spatially joined.

FLOOR PLAN

Because the kitchen is so small, the architect
decided to integrate it into the living room
with two sliding doors in the extremes to serve
the dining room and the exit to the terrace.

The filters in the apartment integrate different storage zones like the shelving that separates the bedroom from the living room or the bookcase next to the bed. Therefore, the permeability has also been established according to which areas are used the most.

The dining room is framed by the meeting of the main room and the bedroom, between the routing of the ceiling's plaster and the wood treatment of the bedroom's enclosure.

Shelving that does not
reach the ceiling separates
the bedroom from a small
office that acts as the
bedroom's anteroom.

There are different areas for storing books in
the bedroom that are perfectly integrated in the
dwelling. Under the large window and along its
entire length there is a large continuous row.

The bathroom is a reflection of the careful
treatment of this apartment. The bath is
separated by a glass partition that fits against
the sink in the bathroom area, lit by a luminous
box. A wood box built into the wall with the mirror
also acts as the bathroom closet and makes
the bathroom seem larger, and the radiator
reflected in the mirror acts as a towel rail and
as a separating element in a storage area.

The kitchen, parallel to the living room and perpendicular to the façade, has a very linear geometry. Being a little narrow, it empties out toward the living room through sliding doors that, when closed, look like a wood parameter, aligned with the cooking area's slate floor.

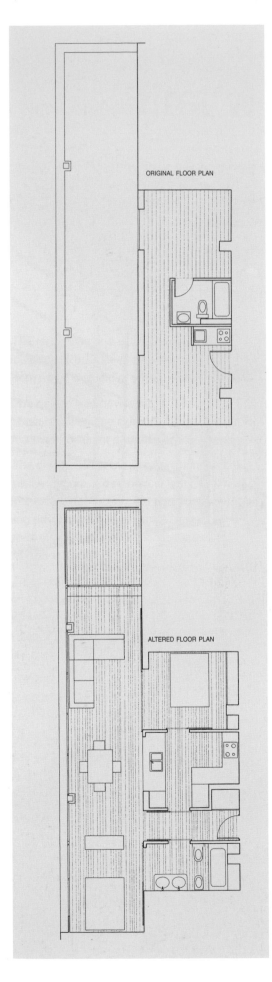

ORIGINAL FLOOR PLAN

ALTERED FLOOR PLAN

The original apartment only consisted of two small rooms separated by a kitchen, bathroom nucleus, and a large exterior terrace. The architects decided to cover part of the terrace and completely change the apartment's distribution to obtain a very modern, luminous, and functional space.

The bathroom is made up of two entrances with equipped with sliding doors from the floor to the ceiling. One of these entrances is smaller and for general use and can be reached from the hall. The other is larger and connected to the bedroom, visually extending it. When these two entrances are closed, the bathroom appears like one white compact block, but, when they are open, the space flows between the rooms.

The new distribution creates a peripheral route around the kitchen's nucleus, visually joining the rooms by the sliding doors. You can partially or entirely see the apartment from each one of these rooms.

When the sliding doors are open, they expand the
room's area toward the adjoining room, creating an
open space. But when they are closed, the space
is fragmented to maintain the inhabitants' intimacy.

From the main bedroom, all of the apartment's rooms are perceived at an angle: hall, bathroom, kitchen, and living/dining room. With the sliding doors covering the entire height of the apartment, the space's vertical longitude is visually lengthened, making it seem higher than it actually is, and creating a pleasant feeling of spaciousness.

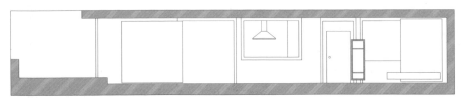

CROSS-SECTION

From the bathroom and second bedroom the sequence of bathroom-hallway-kitchen-bedroom circulation gives rise to an alternative route around the kitchen. The location of the linked paths harmonizes with the lined-up doors in the style of the Italian Renaissance palaces.

The bedroom is separated from the main living/dining room space by a closet that does not break the continuity or spaciousness of the apartment. This main space is perpendicularly linked to the rest of the apartment's rooms by wide perforations or large sliding doors.

From the hall, lit by windows located at the back of the house, part of the dining room, bedroom, and bathroom can be made out, giving an idea of the possible permeability present of the whole design.

The floor was made with stacked roble boards of different widths, which increased the feeling of spaciousness. The parameters and doors were painted white to emphasize the light that is shaded by the awning/parasols located all along the house's exterior.